And Adam Knew Eve

And Adam Knew Eve

A Dictionary of Sex in the Bible

Ronald L. Ecker

Hodge & Braddock, *Publishers*

AND ADAM KNEW EVE
A Dictionary of Sex in the Bible

Library of Congress Catalog Card Number: 94-78430

ISBN 0-9636512-4-2

First Edition

For Kathy and Karen

Preface

The biblical Hebrews, given God's commandment to "be fruitful and multiply" (Gen. 2:28), had what Drorah O'Donnell Setel has alliteratively called a "preoccupation with procreation." That's why many of the stories and other passages in the Bible involve sex, and why many of these, unheard of in sermons and Sunday school lessons, remain little known anong laity.

The purpose of *And Adam Knew Eve* is to inform as well as hopefully to entertain, by gathering from the biblical text all sexually related stories, concepts, and laws, and presenting them, concisely but with attention to context, in convenient dictionary form. Sexually related material comprises overall such a significant portion of scripture that some knowledge of it is essential both in appreciating the Bible as a whole and in understanding the difference in attitude toward sex to be found between the Old and New Testaments.

It is hoped that *And Adam Knew Eve* will also help better acquaint the general reader with the problem that biblical interpreters—in particular feminist scholars—face in the sometimes physically abusive treatment of women under the patriarchal system that so controlled women's lives, sexual and otherwise, in the biblical world.

The term "Bible" in this work includes the Hebrew Bible or Old Testament, the New Testament of Christianity, and the Apocrypha (books, such as Judith, Susanna, and Tobit, included in the Catholic Bible but not in the Hebrew or Protestant Christian canons). Books from the Pseudepigrapha (literally "falsely inscribed," anonymous Jewish and Christian works, usually self-attributed to worthies such as Enoch—quoted in Jude 14—and Peter) are occasionally cited for the light they may shed on the canonical texts.

In quoting lines or verses of scripture, I have used the King James Version (KJV) of the Bible for the enduring quality of its language. The only exceptions are my own translation of lines from the Apocrypha and a couple of other lines for clarity. Occasionally a single word or phrase from the Revised Standard Version (RSV) or the New Revised Standard Version (NRSV) is cited where translation is debated by scholars. For historical dates I have used B.C.E. (Before the Common Era) instead of B.C., and C.E. (Common Era) instead of A.D.

As with most dictionaries, the subject entries in *And Adam Knew Eve* are arranged alphabetically. At the end of most entries, however, there is the sign ⇒ followed by the title of the entry that comes next chronologically. This is for the benefit of those who may wish to read entries in chronological order. The order so indicated reflects the sequence in which biblical events are supposed to have occurred, irrespective of the order of books in the Bible. The entry on Ezra, for example, is followed by the entry on Judith, as both characters live in post-exilic times, even though the apocryphal Judith is generally considered fictitious. Not included in this order, of course, are the entries on general subjects such as adultery and marriage that have no historical sequence. (The chronological entries begin with "Adam and Eve," and end with "Babylon," from the book of Revelation.)

I wish to express my deep appreciation to Richard H. Hiers, professor of religion at the University of Florida, for graciously taking the time to read this work in its galley form. His comments and suggestions were invaluable in the final editing of *And Adam Knew Eve*.

CONTENTS

And Adam Knew Eve

A

AARON AND THE GOLDEN CALF

When Moses, communing with the Lord God in a cloud atop
Mount Sinai, is gone for forty days, the children of Israel,
encamping below, turn to Moses' brother Aaron. "Up, make
for us gods who shall lead us," the people tell him, "for we do
not know what has become of Moses, the man who led us up
out of the land of Egypt."

Aaron, not yet aware that God on the mountain has ap-
pointed him head of the Israelite priesthood, is all too eager to
oblige them. He collects their golden earrings and, using a
graving tool, fashions a molten calf, a young bull being a symbol
of fertility in ancient Near Eastern cults. Building an altar for
the golden calf, Aaron proclaims a feast, at which the Hebrew
people eat and drink and then rise up "to play" (Hebrew *kaheq*,
the same word used for Isaac's sexual "sporting" with Rebekah
in Gen. 26:8).

Moses, arriving with two tablets inscribed by the finger of
God, is so incensed by the orgiastic scene that he throws down
the tablets and breaks them.

"What did this people do to you," Moses asks Aaron, "that
you have brought upon them so great a sin?"

"You know the people," says Aaron, "they are set on evil."
Aaron allows that he accepted their gold, which he threw into
the fire, "and there came out this calf."

Moses punishes all guilty parties through a trial by ordeal:
he burns the calf, grinds it to powder, puts the powder in water,

and makes everyone drink it. God then sends a plague for good measure. It will not be the last time, though, that the children of Israel turn to idols. (See BAALIM AND ASHTAROTH and HARLOTRY: "A-WHORING AFTER OTHER GODS.")

(EXODUS 32)   ⇒ COZBI AND ZIMRI

ABIGAIL AND DAVID

Young David is an outlaw, running from Israel's King Saul, when he first meets Abigail. Though "beautiful" and intelligent ("of good understanding"), Abigail is married to a "churlish" rancher named Nabal. David and his men are on their way to kill Nabal for refusing to provision David's gang ("Who," Nabal wanted to know, "is David?"), when Abigail comes out to meet David with provisions and apologies. She tells David to disregard Nabal, whose name means "fool" in Hebrew. "As his name is," says Abigail, "so is he; Nabal is his name, and folly is with him." She adds that God will surely make David king of Israel, and she asks that David "remember thine handmaid" when that time comes.

Her words please David, who tells Abigail, "Blessed be the Lord God of Israel, which sent thee this day to meet me," for had Abigail not interceded, there would not be a single man— "any that pisseth against the wall," as the outlaw puts it—left alive at Nabal's place.

When Abigail's fool of a husband soon dies anyway, David, saying "Blessed be the Lord," can't wait to send the widow a marriage proposal, and Abigail can't wait to accept: we are told that she "hasted, and arose, and rode upon an ass ... and became (David's) wife." Abigail bears David a son, who is named either Chileab (2 Sam. 3:3) or Daniel (1 Chr. 3:1).

David also has a sister named Abigail, whose husband is named either Ithra the Israelite (2 Sam. 17:25) or Jether the Ishmaelite (1 Chr. 2:17). To appreciate how we know of this marriage, one must first understand that there are no words in

biblical Hebrew specifically for husband and wife (see MAR-
RIAGE). That a man and a woman are married must therefore
be determined by context. (Abigail the widow becomes David's
"woman" [ishah], in context meaning wife.) 2 Sam. 17:25 em-
ploys a unique way of providing context: Ithra (aka Jether), we
are simply told, is the man who "went in to Abigail." (The
Hebrew verb bo is translated "went in to"; see LOVEMAKING:
TO KNOW IN THE BIBLICAL SENSE.)   (1 SAM. 25:5-42)

⇒ DAVID AND MICHAL

ABISHAG THE SHUNAMMITE

In his old age King David is so infirm that a search is conducted
throughout Israel for a suitable young virgin to serve as his
nurse. Selected is Abishag the Shunammite, a "fair damsel" who
is brought to David and cares for him. Abishag lies in his bosom,
keeping the old man warm, but the king—probably not from any
lack of desire—doesn't "know her."
    When David dies, his son Solomon, succeeding to the
throne, inherits Abishag as part of the royal harem. Solomon's
brother Adonijah (described as "a very handsome man"), having tried to set himself up as king while the impotent David still
lived, won't leave well enough alone. Adonijah sends the queen
mother Bathsheba to Solomon to ask that the king give him
Abishag the Shunammite in marriage.
    One might think that Solomon could easily spare Abishag,
special though she may be, as she is but one of his seven hundred
concubines. But Solomon views Adonijah's request as nothing
short of treason, for taking another man's concubine is openly
to challenge his authority. (See CONCUBINES: "MANY
STRANGE WOMEN.") "Ask for him the kingdom also," Solomon wisecracks to Bathsheba, and has Adonijah put to death.
(1 KINGS 1-2:25)   ⇒ SOLOMON AND HIS "OUTLANDISH WOMEN"

ABORTION/MISCARRIAGE

See CONCEPTION: "MADE IN SECRET."

ABRAHAM AND SARAH

At the age of seventy-five, a Semitic nomad named Abram (Hebrew "exalted father") takes his wife Sarai (Hebrew "princess") and nephew Lot from Mesopotamia to the land of Canaan, where the Hebrew God Yahweh tells him, "Unto thy seed will I give this land." The land is soon hit with a famine, prompting Abram and Sarai to take refuge in Egypt. There Abram has Sarai claim to be his sister, for he fears someone might kill him to take his wife, still beautiful at age sixty-five. (Thus Abram's own safety comes first, irrespective of what will happen to his "sister.") Sarai is in fact his half-sister, according to Gen. 20:12, which means that she and Abram are only half lying—but which also means that their marriage is incestuous. (See INCEST.)

When the Pharoah's men lay eyes on her, Sarai is "taken into Pharoah's house"—that is, added to the royal harem—while Abram prospers, given livestock and servants by Pharoah. However, Yahweh sends plagues upon Pharoah, who, learning the truth about Sarai, tells Abram, "Behold thy wife, take her, and go thy way." Abram takes her, along with all that the Pharoah has given him.

Later Abram and Sarai, whom God renames Abraham and Sarah, reprise this sister act in the town of Gerar, with Sarah, still beautiful at age ninety, taken into the harem of King Abimelech. The problem of adultery, implicit in the Pharoah episode, is averted this time: Yahweh tells Abimelech the truth about Sarah in a dream before the king makes any advances ("Abimelech had not come near her"). Still, God punishes the king, afflicting all his house with infertility be-cause Sarah is there, till Abraham intercedes—after receiving more livestock and servants—and takes her off the king's hands. When the childless Sarah is seventy-six, she offers to eighty-six-year-old Abraham her Egyptian handmaid Hagar. "Go into my maid," Sarah says, "that I might have children by her." (On surrogate child-bearing, see CONCUBINES.) Abraham does as he's told, and Hagar conceives, bearing Ishmael, "a wild ass of a man." (Conflict ensues between Hagar and Sarah, with Abraham eventually sending away Hagar and Ishmael at Sarah's insistence. Ishmael, who will have twelve sons, is traditionally the progenitor of the Arabs.)

When Abraham is ninety-nine, he receives from Yahweh his new name (meaning "father of many nations") and the order to undergo circumcision, sign of God's everlasting covenant with Abraham and his seed. Yet when God tells Abraham that Sarah will be "a mother of nations," his response is to fall down laughing. Sarah laughs too, albeit more discreetly, when she overhears an angel tell Abraham that she will bear a child. But Yahweh has the last laugh ("Is anything too hard for the Lord?"): on the return from Gerar, Sarah conceives and bears Isaac (whose name means "one who laughs") in her ninetieth year.

After Sarah dies at age one hundred and twenty-seven, Abraham has six more children by a wife named Keturah, plus sons by an unspecified number of concubines, before dying at one hundred and seventy-five, "in a good old age."
(GEN. 12:5-20; 16-18; 20; 21:1-5; 25:1-8.)   ⇒ SODOM(Y) AND GOMORRAH

ABSALOM AND THE TEN CONCUBINES

King David's oldest son Amnon rapes his half-sister Tamar, for which her full brother Absalom has Amnon murdered. (See AMNON AND TAMAR). David mourns Amnon's death, and Absalom finds it advisable to get out of Jerusalem, spending three years in exile.

After his return, the handsome and cunning Absalom leads a rebellion against his father. Now it's David who gets out of

Jerusalem, leaving ten concubines behind in the palace to keep house. Absalom asks Ahithophel, a royal counsellor turned traitor, what to do next. "Go into thy father's concubines," Ahithophel tells him. Such an ostentatious power play will show the people who is now in charge (see CONCUBINES). When Ahithophel speaks, all listen. A tent is accordingly spread on top of the house, and Absalom has sexual intercourse with David's ten concubines "in the sight of all Israel." (This fulfills a prophecy of Nathan following David's adultery with Bathsheba and the killing of her husband Uriah: a neighbor, God tells David through the prophet, "shall lie with thy wives in the sight of this sun.")

The rebellion nonetheless fails, with Ahithophel hanging himself and Absalom dying after riding under an oak tree and getting his hairy head caught in the branches. David thus loses another unscrupulous son ("O my son Absalom, my son, my son Absalom! would God I had died for thee, O Absalom, my son, my son!"). As for the ten concubines, David never again has sex with them. The king keeps them shut up, "in widowhood, unto the day of their death."   (2 SAM. 12:11, 13:1-20:3)

⇒ ABISHAG THE SHUNAMMITE

ABSTINENCE/ASCETICISM

See JESUS CHRIST: THERE AIN'T NO SEX IN HEAVEN; LOVEMAKING: TO KNOW IN THE BIBLICAL SENSE; PAUL: "BETTER TO MARRY THAN TO BURN"; *and* VIRGINITY: "THE BRIDEGROOM REJOICETH."

ADAM AND EVE

When God creates the first man (Hebrew *adam*) and woman (named *Hawwah* ["Eve"], similar to Hebrew *hayyah*, "life"), he commands them, "Be fruitful and multiply." It should follow, then, that Adam and Eve engage in sex early on. The book of Genesis, however, is silent on this question. The couple remains childless while in the Garden of Eden, and until their loss of innocence Adam and Eve are not even aware of their nakedness. Some interpreters take this to mean that Adam and Eve before the Fall are not aware of their sexuality. But that makes nonsense of the divine command to procreate. It also suggests that sex is somehow to be associated with the Fall and is thus tainted with sin and shame. Such a view reflects a later ascetic Christian, not a biblical Hebrew, attitude toward human sexuality. (See LOVEMAKING and VIRGINITY.)

One can speculate, based on Gen. 1:27, that Adam and Eve were originally one androgynous being—"God created man in his own image, . . . male and female created he them"—meant to reproduce in some asexual way. But again this associates sex with the couple's Fall (their original state being androgyny or asexuality), an un-Hebrew notion that also conflicts with Genesis 2, according to which man and woman were not created simultaneously.

Perhaps Genesis makes no mention of Adam and Eve making love in the Garden of Eden because it is taken for granted. James Barr, in *The Garden of Eden and the Hope of Immortality*, points out that there was no reason, given the acceptance of sexuality as normal in ancient Hebrew culture, for the couple to abstain. In the noncanonical book of Jubilees (3:6), Adam and Eve have sexual relations as soon as God introduces them. It is literally love at first sight. According to rabbinic tradition, Eve is not even Adam's first wife. His first wife is Lilith, who leaves him because during sexual intercourse Adam won't let her be on top. (For more on this failed relationship, see GENDER: "MALE AND FEMALE CREATED HE THEM.")

Sex, in any case, has nothing to do with Adam and Eve's Fall from grace in Genesis. Their sin is one of disobedience, specifically eating fruit from the "tree of the knowledge of good and evil," that is, reaching for godlike knowledge ("ye shall be as gods," the serpent tells Eve, "knowing good and evil" [Gen.

3:5]) (see Gaster). Eve, tempted by the serpent to partake of the fruit, gets blamed by Adam ("she gave me of the tree," Adam tells God, "and I did eat," as if Eve had a choice but poor Adam didn't). (The woman is given all the blame also by the early Christian church; see PAUL.) God punishes them both, with the punishment of Eve being pain in childbirth ("in sorrow thou shalt bring forth children") and unequal status ("thy desire," God tells her, "will be to thy husband, and he shall rule over thee"; see GENDER).

The first sex act described in the Bible comes after the departure from Eden: "And Adam knew Eve his wife" ("to know," Hebrew *yada*, being a euphemism for sexual intercourse), "and she conceived, and bare Cain." As Barr notes, intercourse is here described for the first time because it is the first time that a child is produced. Adam and Eve then have a second son, Abel, and when Adam is one hundred and thirty years old he knows Eve again, fathering Seth.

How many times Adam knows Eve after that, or how many more wives Adam knows, is unknown, but he begets "sons and daughters " for eight hundred more years. (GEN. 1:26-5:5) ⇒CAIN

ADULTERY: "Fire in the Bosom"

The seventh of the ten commandments ("Thou shalt not commit adultery" [Ex. 20:15, Deut. 5:18]) does not refer to adultery as generally thought of today. In the Old Testament a married man, but not a married woman, could have sex outside of marriage and not be an adulterer. Under the Hebrew patriarchal system, a man commits adultery only if the sex is with another man's wife or virginal betrothed—in effect a property crime analogous, as Judith Romney Wegner puts it, to stealing the other man's cow. (On women as property, see GENDER.)

The penalty for adultery is death for both parties (Lev. 20:10; Deut. 22:22). In the case of a betrothed virgin, she is considered guilty of consent, and is therefore to die with the man, if the incident occurred in the city and she did not scream for help (Deut. 22:23-27).

The book of Numbers (5:12-31) provides for a trial by ordeal in cases where a man suspects his wife of adultery but has no proof. The man, being moved by a "spirit of jealousy," shall bring his wife and a "jealousy offering" to the priest, who will mix holy water with dust from the temple floor and make the woman drink it. If she has "lain with" no man but her husband, this "bitter water" will not cause "the curse," but if she is guilty of adultery, "her belly shall swell, and her thigh shall rot," and she will be "a curse among her people."

Adultery is often used in the Old Testament as a metaphor for the unfaithfulness toward God of the people of Israel and Judah, who "go a-whoring after other gods" (Judg. 2:17). God speaks in Jer. 3:8 of divorcing Israel for her adultery, then "her treacherous sister Judah . . . played the harlot also." The prophet Hosea deliberately marries an adulteress to dramatize God's dilemma with the backsliding children of Israel.

The adultery metaphor takes its most graphic form in Ezekiel 23, describing in detail the allegorical promiscuity of the sisters Oholah and Oholibah, adulterous wives of Yahweh.

The book of Proverbs extols the wisdom of avoiding adulterous situations. "Can a man take fire in his bosom," it asks, "and his clothes not be burned?" (Adultery "is a fire," says Job [31:12], "that consumeth to destruction.") The commandment against adultery, we are told in Proverbs, helps "keep thee from the evil woman." The book describes "a young man devoid of understanding" who is lured to the house of "a woman with the attire of an harlot." Catching him and kissing him, she says, "I have decked my bed . . . with fine linen of Egypt . . . Come, let us take our fill of love until the morning," for "(my husband) is not at home." But though "stolen waters are sweet," says Proverbs, "he that goeth in to his neighbour's wife . . . lacketh understanding," and the house of the adulteress "is the way to hell" (6:23-32, 7:4-27).

Not only is the seventh commandment reaffirmed in the New Testament (Matt. 19:18, Luke 18:20, Rom. 13:9, James

2:11), but adultery is broadened to include even thinking about committing it. "Whoever looks at a woman with lust," says Jesus Christ in Matt. 5:28, "has committed adultery with her already in his heart." Jesus also states that adultery includes remarriage after divorce (Matt. 19:9, Luke 16:18).

Still, one of the Bible's best-known passages speaks of forgiveness for adultery (as for all sin), not punishment. Scribes and Pharisees bring to Jesus "a woman taken in adultery, in the very act" (John 8:3-11). They remind him that an adulteress should be stoned, "but what do you say?"

"Let him who is without sin among you," replies Jesus, "cast the first stone." The accusers leave one by one, leaving none to condemn her. "Neither do I condemn you," Jesus tells the adulteress. "Go, and sin no more."

AHAB AND JEZEBEL

King Ahab of Israel does "more to provoke the Lord God of Israel to anger than all the kings of Israel before him." In particular he serves the Canaanite fertility god Baal, reflecting the influence of his Phoenician wife Jezebel, daughter of the king of Sidon. Jezebel keeps Ahab "stirred up," and the prophets of Baal and of the goddess Asherah (eight hundred and fifty in all) "eat at Jezebel's table."

Ahab's and Jezebel's daughter Athaliah marries King Jehoram of Judah, where Baalism is then also promoted. (Jezebel's Ahab is not to be confused, incidentally, with the book of Jeremiah's Ahab, one of two false prophets who "commit adultery with their neighbor's wives" and are "roasted in the fire" by the king of Babylon.)

King Ahab is killed in battle while disguised as a common soldier. Some harlots wash themselves in his blood. Ahab's and Jezebel's son Joram becomes king after the short reign of an older brother. Jehu, a rebel leader intent on destroying the house of Ahab full of Jezebel's "whoredoms" and "witchcrafts," assassinates Joram (and, while he's at it, Ahab's grandson Ahaziah, king of Judah). Jehu then goes after Jezebel. On hearing he's coming, the queen mother paints her face, adorns her head, and looks out at an upper window. (Thus she is pictured, notes Mary Chilton Calloway, as a whore.) "Is it peace, you Zimri?" she asks Jehu arriving below. (The question is rhetorical, since Zimri, as she immediately notes, "murdered his master"; see 1 Kings 16:8-12.)

"Who is on my side?" Jehu shouts, and "two or three eunuchs" appear at the window. "Throw her down," Jehu commands, and they do. After trampling Jezebel with his chariot, Jehu goes in for a bite to eat. He gives orders too late for "this cursed woman" to be buried, as dogs devour Jezebel's body except for the skull, feet, and palms. (This fulfills, for the most part, a prophecy of Elijah in 1 Kings 21:23.) Now her carcass, Jehu notes, "shall be dung on the face of the field."

Jebezel lives on, though, as a synonym for a wicked woman. The book of Revelation complains of a "Jezebel," calling herself a prophetess, who leads people in the church at Thyatira "to commit fornication." "I will cast her into a bed," says Saint John, "and them that commit adultery with her into great tribulation, except they repent their deeds."

(1 KINGS 16:29-33; 18:19; 21:25; 22:30-38; 2 KINGS 9:16-37; 10:1; REV. 2:20-22)

⇒ ATHALIAH AND JEHORAM

AHASUERUS AND ESTHER

See ESTHER: "THE MAIDEN WHO PLEASES THE KING."

AMNON AND TAMAR

King David's oldest son Amnon is lovesick, growing "lean day by day," for the object of his desire is Tamar. She is his virgin half-sister, so "it is hard for him to do anything to her." But his cousin Jonadab, "a very subtle man," suggests that Amnon pretend to be sick in bed, and that when his father David visits him he ask that Tamar be sent to feed him. Amnon follows this advice, playing sick and requesting that Tamar come make him "a couple of cakes."

Tamar dutifully makes some pancakes and brings them into Amnon's chamber. The pancakes are apparently heart-shaped, like Old Testament valentines. (The noun "pancakes" and the verb for making them in Hebrew are both related to *lebab*, Hebrew "heart" [see Brockington and Hackett]. The verb is used in the Song of Solomon [4:9] as "Thou hast ravished" [literally made pancakes of] "my heart.")

Amnon, who has sent everyone else away, takes hold of Tamar's hand. "Come lie with me, my sister," he tells her, but Tamar says, "Nay, my brother, do not force me." She asks that Amnon instead speak to the king, "for he will not withhold me from thee." (Laws recorded in Lev. 18:9,11, 20:17, and Deut. 27:22, prohibiting marriage between a half-brother and sister, may not yet exist when this story takes place.) But Amnon, "being stronger than she," rapes Tamar.

Immediately after this deed Amnon hates her, and tells Tamar, "Arise, be gone." She says there is no cause, that to send her away is worse than what he has already done. (As scholar Jo Ann Hackett points out, Tamar may here have in mind the law [Ex. 22:16] that a man must marry a virgin whom he has seduced.) Amnon calls his servant and orders him to "put this woman out" and "bolt the door after her."

Tamar goes to live, a "desolate" woman, in the house of her full brother Absalom, who resolves that Amnon will pay. Two years later, while Amnon drinks merrily with his brothers at a sheepshearing festival, he is murdered by Absalom's servants. (Absalom's other brothers immediately haul ass—each "got up on his mule and fled.")

Absalom later has a daughter, "a beautiful woman," named after his sister Tamar.   (2 SAM. 13:1-29)

⇒ ABSALOM AND THE TEN CONCUBINES

ASHERAH: The Lord God's Lady?

The goddess Asherah was the consort of El ("god"), the supreme god of Canaan and father of the popular Baal. In the Bible her name often appears as *ha asherah*, meaning "the" asherah. In such instances the reference is not to the goddess but to a symbol of her, an object (in the plural *asherim*) that was apparently a sacred pole, tree, or group of trees (hence the translation "groves") at Israelite sanctuaries or "high places" as well as by altars of Baal. The erecting of *asherim* was among the "evil" deeds of kings like Ahab and Manasseh, and cutting the things down was a regular chore of "right" kings like Hezekiah and Josiah.

The presence of Asherah or her symbol at places where Yahweh, the biblical God of the Hebrews, was worshipped raises the question of whether the Canaanite goddess was considered also to be the consort of Yahweh. We know from references to "the sons of God" (Gen. 6:1-4; Job 1:6, 2:1, 38:7), "the host of heaven" (1 Kings 22:19), "angels" (Gen. 19:1; Ps. 103:20), and God's statement "Let us make man in our image" (Gen. 1:26), that Yahweh was not alone in his heaven. We know also that Yahweh supplanted the Canaanite El to the extent that God's other names in the Hebrew Bible include El, El Elyon ("God Most High"), El Shaddai ("God Almighty"), and the (originally) plural form Elohim (as in Gen. 1:1). But did Yahweh take El's woman too?

The answer may well be found, appropriately enough, in some graffiti, inscriptions dating from the eighth century B.C.E., found on walls and storage jars at two sites, Khirbet el-Kom and Kuntillet Ajrud, in Israel. (See Dever's *Recent Archaeological Discoveries and Biblical Research*.) The graffiti includes blessings such as "I bless you by Yahweh of Samaria and by his asherah," and "I bless you by Yahweh of Teiman and by his asherah." Does this mean by Yahweh and by his goddess? Or is it saying "by Yahweh and by his sacred pole"?

All we may safely assume at this point has been well put by

the French epigrapher André Lemaire: "Whatever an asherah is, Yahweh had one!" (See also BAALIM AND ASHTAROTH and YAHWEH: "THY MAKER IS THINE HUSBAND.")

ASHTAROTH/ASHTORETH/ASTARTE

See BAALIM AND ASHTORETH.

ATHALIAH AND JEHORAM

King Jehoram of Judah (whose name ironically means "God is exalted") leads his people into idolatry—often biblically called "a-whoring after other gods"—with a vigor rivaling that of Ahab and Jezebel, the rulers of Israel to the north. Jehoram even has his own Jezebel, Athaliah, who is in fact Ahab's and Jezebel's daughter. Like her Phoenician mother in Israel, Athaliah in Judah promotes the cult of the fertility god Baal.

None of this is lost on the prophet Elijah, who writes Jehoram a nasty letter comparing the way the king causes "Judah and the inhabitants of Jerusalem to go a-whoring" to "the whoredoms of the house of Ahab."

For his evil ways, Elijah says in the letter, King Jehoram will have "a great sickness" that will make his "bowels fall out."

Few deserve bowel trouble more than Jehoram, who in addition to his "whoring" has slain his six brothers, as real or imagined threats to his power. At the age of forty, his bowels fall out as predicted and Jehoram dies "of sore diseases."

This doesn't faze Athaliah, who proceeds to guide Jehoram's successor, their son Ahaziah, "in the ways of the house of Ahab." When Ahaziah is slain by the rebel Jehu, Athaliah has all her grandsons slain (so she thinks) and assumes the throne herself. She is the only woman ever to be the sole royal power in either Israel or Judah.

But one of Athaliah's grandsons, Joash, has been secretly

saved by his aunt Jehoshabeath. The aunt's husband, Jehoiada the priest, now leads a revolt. The people crown seven-year-old Joash as king, and Athaliah is put to the sword. They tear down the temple of her beloved fertility god Baal, kill Baal's priest Mattan before the altars, and smash the god's images to pieces.

The priest Jehoiada continues to look after Athaliah's grandson, King Joash. As soon as the king's old enough, Jehoiada finds him two wives, by whom the king, we are told, "begat sons and daughters." When Jehoiada dies, however, the people under King Joash again go a-whoring, serving "Asherah and idols" (see ASHERAH and BAALIM AND ASHTAROTH.)

(2 KINGS 8:16-25; 9:27; 11:1-12:3; 2 CHR. 21-23, 24:3,17-18)   ⇒ HOSEA

B

BAALIM AND ASHTAROTH

When the children of Israel went "a-whoring after other gods" (Judg. 2:17), as they often did, they went generally after Baal and Astarte. Baal ("lord"), known also as Hadad, was the Canaanite god of fertility. He had many local manifestations, such as Baal of Peor (Num. 25:3), and Baal-berith, "lord of the covenant," at Shechem (Judg. 8:33), hence the plural form Baalim. A storm god, Baal died in the spring, wailed over and buried by his consort, the love and war goddess Anat (compare the women mourning for Hadad-rimmon, i.e. Baal, in Zech. 12:11, and those weeping for Tammuz, the dying fertility god of Babylon, in Ezek. 8:14). But in the fall Baal revived, vanquishing Mot, the god of death and drought, and bringing with him the autumn rains. In a graphic but fragmentary text from Canaanite Ugarit, the triumphant Baal and Anat make love, with Anat giving birth to a buffalo. (See Pritchard's *Ancient Near Eastern Texts.* On other dying and reviving gods of the ancient world— Osiris in Egypt, Adonis in Syria, Attis in Phrygia and Rome—see Frazer's *The New Golden Bough.*)

Astarte (Babylon's Ishtar, Sumer's Inanna), love goddess of the Phoenicians, is named in the Bible Ashtoreth, combining the consonants from Astarte and the vowels from *boshet*, Hebrew "shame." She was also known and worshipped in Judah as the Queen of Heaven (Jer. 7:16-20; 44:15-28; see Ackerman). Among others King Solomon, we are told, "went after Ashtoreth" (1 Kings 11:5). In the Bible the plural form, Ashtaroth, is more frequently used, to cover pagan goddesses generally. (See also ASHERAH.)

It has long been assumed that sacred prostitution was practiced in the worship of Baalim, Ashtaroth, and other such deities in the ancient Near East. But while cultic sex in fertility rites would not be surprising, there is no real evidence that ritual sex existed outside of annual sacred marriages, intended to promote fertility, between Mesopotamian kings and female partners standing (or lying) in for the love goddess. The marriage of the Sumerian king, representing the god Dumuzi (Babylon's Tammuz), to the goddess Inanna is textually preserved in sacred marriage songs such as "Plow My Vulva" (see Frymer-Kensky's *In the Wake of the Goddesses*, and Wolkstein and Kramer's *Inanna*). On the issue of cultic sex in the Bible, see PROSTITUTION: IS NOTHING SACRED?

BABYLON, "THE MOTHER OF HARLOTS"

In the book of Revelation, John of Patmos, writing probably during the reign of the Roman emperor Domitian (81-96 C.E.), refers to Rome as Babylon, "the great whore who sits upon many waters." John describes her as a bejeweled woman "with whom the kings of the earth have committed fornication." From her "wine of fornication" the inhabitants of the earth have become drunk, and she herself is "drunk with the blood of the saints and the blood of the martyrs of Jesus." She is seated on a scarlet beast with ten horns (unidentified powers within the empire), in her hand a golden cup "full of the abominations and filthiness of her fornication." According to Seneca (cited by Nigel Turner), harlots in Rome wore their names on their foreheads. John's drunken harlot has a name upon hers: "Babylon the Great, the Mother of Harlots and of the Earth's Abominations."

John prophesies that the beast with its horns will "hate the whore, and shall make her desolate and naked, and shall eat her flesh, and burn her with fire." Then all the kings of the earth "who have committed fornication and lived deliciously with her, shall bewail her" upon seeing "the smoke of her burning."

John's great whore mixes the metaphor of harlotry, used so often for idolatry in the Old Testament, with the prophet Jeremiah's treatment of the actual city of Babylon ("O thou that dwellest upon many waters"[51:13], referring to the Euphrates river and canal system). The whore's golden cup and wine of fornication recalls Jer. 51:7, in which Babylon is "a golden cup in the Lord's hand, that made all the earth drunken."

Such lurid reworking by John of Jeremiah's material suggests at least some design behind what has been called the "kaleidoscopic" nature of John's visions—though certainly it may still be doubted, to quote the Rev. Turner, if "John himself really understood all that he wrote." (REV. 17, 18:9)

⇒ ADAM AND EVE

BATHSHEBA: "I Am with Child"

One evening King David takes a stroll on the roof of his palace. From the roof he sees "a woman washing herself," and she is beautiful to behold. David inquires about her identity, and is told, "Is not this Bathsheba, the daughter of Eliam, the wife of Uriah the Hittite?" (No, not according to the Chronicler, who calls her Bathshua, the daughter of Ammiel [1 Chr. 3:5]—but then see also the Chronicler's confusion under ABIGAIL AND DAVID.)

Bathsheba's husband, Uriah the Hittite, is away fighting the Ammonites for God and country. David sends for Bathsheba, she comes, and they have what David perhaps intends to be a one-night stand. (He ignores the fact, if she tells him, that she's ritually "unclean," being still in her seven-day purification period (see MENSTRUATION: SEVEN LONELY DAYS.) But Bathsheba conceives and sends David the news: "I am with child."

David sends for Uriah the Hittite, ostensibly for a report on the war. After hearing Uriah's report, David tells him, "Go down to your house, wash your feet"—in other words, go spend

some time with Bathsheba. The Hittite leaves the king's presence, but instead of going down to his house he spends the night
with the palace guards.

When David finds this out the next day, he calls Uriah in.
"Why," David asks, "did you not go down to your house?" The
Hittite replies that his fellow warriors are out camping some-
where in the field. "Shall I then go to my house," Uriah asks,
"to eat and to drink, and to lie with my wife?"—which is exactly
what David wants him to do. Uriah refuses to do it. (Uriah is not
just objecting to having it better than his fellows. As a warrior
who must return to battle, he is concerned, as noted in Meeks,
with ritual purity [Deut. 23:9; 1 Sam. 21:4-5].)

That night David gets the man drunk, but again the Hittite
goes out and sleeps with the royal guards instead of going home
to Bathsheba.

David gives up. Sending Uriah back to the war, the king
orders that the fellow be placed "in the forefront of the hottest
battle." Sure enough, the pregnant Bathsheba soon is a widow.
After her period of mourning, David has her "fetched to his
house" and marries her.

Bathsheba bears David's son, but Yahweh, the Lord God of
Israel, is displeased by this whole affair. (David, we are told in
1 Kings 15:5, always did right in God's eyes, "save only in the
matter of Uriah the Hittite.") The prophet Nathan conveys
God's angry words to the king: "I will raise up evil against thee
out of thine own house, and I will take thy wives before thine
eyes, and give them unto thy neighbour, and he shall lie with thy
wives in the sight of this sun." (This is a prophecy of the revolt
led by Absalom, David's third son, who will violate David's
harem; see ABSALOM AND THE TEN CONCUBINES.)

David expresses to Nathan his remorse ("I have sinned
against the Lord"), and even composes a penitential psalm (see
the title of Psalm 51): "I was shapen in iniquity," David sings,
"and in sin did my mother conceive me" (Ps. 51:5). Nathan
applauds this, telling David that the Lord "hath put away thy
sin; thou shalt not die." It is the child, says Nathan, who shall die
instead. Yahweh afflicts the child with illness and it dies on the

seventh day.

But the sun, as Ecclesiastes says, also rises. Comforting Bathsheba, David again knows her carnally. She conceives and again bears a son. The child is named Solomon, and he is "loved by the Lord." (2 SAM. 11:2-12:24) ⇒ AMNON AND TAMAR

BENJAMIN: "A Ravenous Wolf"

The concubine of a certain Levite has "played the whore against him" and runs away to Bethlehem to stay in her father's house. The Levite goes to Bethlehem and fetches her, and the two are on their way home when they stop for the night in the town of Gibeah.

Now these are perilous times, for there is still "no king in Israel," and every man does that which is "right in his own eyes." In such times Gibeah may not be the best place for strangers to be spending an evening. It is a town of Benjamin, a tribe named after the youngest son of Jacob. This son's hallmark was rapacity. Benjamin is "a ravenous wolf," as Jacob put it in his deathbed blessing of the lad, "devouring his prey by morning and dividing the spoil by night" (Gen. 49:27).

On this night in Gibeah the Levite and his concubine are enjoying the hospitality of an old man, a fellow non-Benjaminite sojourner, when some of the town's no-goods (literally "sons of Belial," RSV "worthless fellows") "beset the house round about" and beat on the door. They tell the old man to bring out the Levite "that we may know him," meaning that they intend to rape him. (For a very similar incident in the town of Sodom, see SODOM[Y] AND GOMORRAH.)

To make any sense of the old man's reaction, one must take into account both the unequal status of women in the patriarchal society of the biblical Hebrews and the great importance placed in a traditionally nomadic society on hospitality. But even then things in the story turn senseless. To protect his male guest, the old man offers to the men outside his own virgin daughter and the guest's concubine: he tells the fellows to humble them, to do to these two women whatever they like, "but unto this man do not so vile a thing." When the men outside won't listen, the Levite brings his concubine out to them anyway. And "they knew her, and abused her all the night."

The next morning, the Levite rises and finds his concubine lying at the door of the house, with her hands on the threshhold. We are not told if she is dead or alive—but we are told what he says to her: "Up, and let us be going."

When there is no answer, he puts her, dead or alive, on an ass and takes her home. There he takes out a knife (is she still alive?) and butchers her, dividing her into twelve pieces, which he sends to "all the coasts of Israel," to announce the "lewdness and folly" that has been committed.

The other tribes of Israel, in response to the Gibeah atrocity, convene at Mizpah. They agree that none of them will wed any of their daughters to Benjaminites. They also demand that the tribe of Benjamin turn over the Gibeah perpetrators for execution, "to put evil away from Israel." When the Benjaminites refuse, all but six hundred Benjaminite men are wiped out in a war with the other tribes.

Now there's another problem. The ban on marriages with Benjaminites results in a shortage of women for the surviving six hundred men. This is of concern to the other tribes, lest a whole tribe of Israel go extinct.

Taking note of the fact that no one from the town of Jabesh-gilead came to the Mizpah assembly, the tribes decide to send twelve thousand men to Jabesh-gilead, kill every male there and every female who has lain with one, and give all the virgins to Benjamin.

This nets four hundred young virgins for the Benjaminites, which leaves them still two hundred women short. Then someone remembers the annual "feast of the Lord in Shiloh," where "the daughters of Shiloh come out to dance," in a place not far from the "highway." So the tribes send the two hundred still-wifeless Benjaminites to go hide there, with instructions to "catch you every man his wife."

When the daughters of Shiloh start dancing, the hidden Benjaminites rush out of the vineyards and grab the women they want. Going home with new wives, these scions of the ravenous wolf may now repair and replenish their war-ravaged towns. Years later a Benjaminite of Gibeah, Saul, becomes the first king of Israel. (JUDG. 19:1-21:23; 1 SAM. 10:17-27)   ⇒ RUTH

BESTIALITY: No Fit Helper

The biblical penalty for a man or a woman having sex with an animal is death (Exod. 22:19, Lev. 18:30), for "it is confusion" (Lev. 18:23), an egregious mixing of created kinds (see Lev. 19:19 and Deut. 22:9-11). "Cursed be anyone who lies with any kind of beast," says Deuteronomy (27:21), "and all the people shall say 'Amen.' "

Bestiality is listed among the "abominations" of the Canaanites for which they are "spewed out" from the land before the invading Hebrews (Lev. 18). Even the Canaanite gods are not above this "confusion": in a badly damaged text from ancient Ugarit, the fertility god Baal has sex either with a cow or the goddess Anat in bovine form (see Pritchard's *Ancient Near Eastern Texts*).

According to Hebrew tradition, even Adam, the first human being, is confused when his Creator brings him the animals. In Genesis Adam only gives these creatures names. Yet God's whole purpose in creating the beasts, according to the second creation account (Gen. 2), is "to make a helper (Hebrew *ezer*, denoting a companion or partner) fit for (Adam)," which Adam nonetheless fails to find. In rabbinic sources we are told the lengths to which Adam goes to find the right helper: he couples with each female animal, then complains to God, "Every creature but me has a proper mate!" It is only then that God, through trial and error (Adam's first wife Lilith leaves him, and the first Eve is rejected by Adam), creates a fit companion. (See Graves and Patai's *Hebrew Myths*; see also GENDER.)

BILHAH THE HANDMAID

See JACOB AND LABAN'S DAUGHTERS *and* RAPE: "LEWD-NESS AND FOLLY IN ISRAEL."

BIRTH CONTROL/CONTRACEPTION

See CONCEPTION: "MADE IN SECRET."

BOAZ AND RUTH

See RUTH: "AT HIS FEET UNTIL MORNING."

BREASTS: "Milk Out, And Be Delighted"

In the Bible human breasts are symbols of good times, sexual and otherwise, with dry breasts symbolizing calamity. In the latter case, the prophet Hosea (9:14) calls upon God to give his backsliding people "a miscarrying womb and dry breasts." Similarly the New Testament warns mothers of the grief that divine judgment shall bring: "Woe unto them ... that give suck in those days" (Matt. 24:19), and blessed are "the paps which never gave suck" (Luke 23:29). Conversely, Isaiah (66:7-12) foresees a new Jerusalem that will be a loving and bountiful mother, satisfying her children with "the breasts of her consolations," that they may "milk out, and be delighted with the abundance of her glory." In Luke (11:27), a woman tells Jesus, "Blessed is the womb that bare thee, and the paps which thou hast sucked."

The breasts of one's wife are associated with sexual satisfaction in Proverbs ("let her breasts satisfy thee at all times"), so that it should be unnecessary to "embrace the bosom of a stranger"

(5:18-20). Breasts are prominent in the sensuous Song of Solomon: "He shall lie down all night betwixt my breasts (1:13) . . . Thy two breasts are like two young roes that are twins (7:3) . . . Thy breasts shall be as clusters of the vine" (7:7). This romantic imagery contrasts sharply, of course, with the graphic abuse in the parable of the adulterous sisters in Ezekiel: "(In Egypt) were their breasts pressed, and there they bruised the teats of their virginity" (23:3) (see EZEKIEL: TALKING LEWD WOMEN).

We learn in the Song of Solomon (8:8) that breast size was a concern in biblical times just as it is today: "We have a little sister, and she hath no breasts: what shall we do for our sister in the day when she shall be spoken for?"

She who asks the question then boasts: "I am a wall, and my breasts like towers: then was I to his eyes as one that found favour" (8:10).

C

CAIN: The First Hell Ever Raised

Adam and Eve raised Cain, the first human being ever produced by sexual intercourse. ("And Adam knew Eve his wife, and she conceived, and bare Cain." Eve considered him to be a blessing from Yahweh: "I have gotten a man from the Lord." See CONCEPTION: "MADE IN SECRET".) Cain grew up to be a farmer but also the Bible's first murderer, slaying Abel, his sheepherding younger brother. (There is an extrabiblical tradition that Satan, not Adam, was the murderous Cain's father. In this version the devil—in the form of the serpent—tempted Eve into more than the eating of forbidden fruit [Ginzberg 1:107].)

Later "Cain knew his wife; and she conceived, and bare Enoch." This wife is a mystery woman, since at the time of Cain's birth the whole world's population totaled only three (being, of course, Cain and his parents Adam and Eve). Remarkable also is Cain's founding of a city, which implies a considerable number of inhabitants.

The best explanation for such a population explosion from one created couple is the obvious one: inbreeding was originally extensive, indeed unavoidable. Thus Cain in the pseudepigraphical book of Jubilees marries his sister Awan (Adam and Eve's second child, says Jubilees, before Abel), and all the other descendants of Adam, from Seth to Noah, marry sisters or cousins. (GEN. 4:1-17; JUB. 4:9-28) ⇒ METHUSELAH

CANAAN, THE CURSE OF

See NOAH: UNSUNK, AND DRUNK AS A SKUNK.

CANTICLES: "Our Bed is Green"

See SONG OF SOLOMON.

CELIBACY: "Not to Touch a Woman"

See EUNUCHS: "LET HIM ACCEPT IT WHO CAN"; JESUS
CHRIST: THERE AIN'T NO SEX IN HEAVEN; *and* PAUL:
"BETTER TO MARRY THAN TO BURN."

CHILDBIRTH: "A Woman in Travail"

See CONCEPTION: "MADE IN SECRET."

CHRIST: "The Marriage of the Lamb is Come"

See JESUS CHRIST: THERE AIN'T NO SEX IN HEAVEN.

CIRCUMCISION: "Sign of the Covenant"

In Genesis (17:10-12,24), the cutting off of the prepuce or
foreskin of the penis is first ordered by the Hebrew God
Yahweh to symbolize the covenant made between Yahweh and
his people. "Every male among you shall be circumcised," God

tells the Hebrew patriarch Abraham, "and it will be a sign of the covenant between me and you." Abraham dutifully goes first, being circumcised at the age of ninety-nine.

Circumcision as a sign ordained by God may well be an Old Testament explanation for a custom—one not easy to explain, but found in other ancient cultures—that predates the covenant. ("To make a covenant" in biblical Hebrew is literally "to cut a covenant." This use of "to cut," however, is coincidental, referring not to circumcision but to the ritual cutting in two of a sacrificial animal.)

Circumcision may have originated as a rite of passage into manhood. In the Old Testament the practice is sometimes referred to metaphorically. "Circumcise therefore the foreskin of your heart," says Deuteronomy (10:16), "and be no more stiffnecked." The prophet Jeremiah (6:10) describes those who do not listen to the word of God as having uncircumcisd ears.

In the New Testament, there is "no small dissension and disputation" within the Christian community about whether or not circumcision is necessary for salvation. "Except ye be circumcised after the manner of Moses," argue "certain men" from Judea, "ye cannot be saved" (Acts 15:1-2). The Apostle Paul's view, which eventually prevails among Christians, is that "there is no difference between the Jew and the Greek" (Rom. 10:12), that "neither circumcision nor uncircumcision is of any avail, only faith that works by love" (Gal. 5:6). (Paul adds that he would like to see those who disagree with him "cut themselves off" [Gal. 5:12].)

Whatever its origin and spiritual value, circumcision is a custom still practiced by Jews (as well as many non-Jews) today, though critics argue that it is of no real advantage hygenically and is traumatic for the recipient. (Jewish males are circumcised when they are eight days old.) Female circumcision (cutting off of the clitoris and often the labia minora), not mentioned in the Bible but still practiced today in some Arab cultures among others, is mutilation designed to lessen a woman's sexual pleasure, thus presumably helping keep her a virgin till marriage and faithful thereafter.

Notable episodes involving circumcision in the Bible are Zipporah's circumcising of her son to save Moses' life (see MOSES AND ZIPPORAH); the circumcision by Joshua at Gibeath-haaraloth ("hill of the foreskins"), after crossing the Jordan, of all the Hebrew males who had been born in the wilderness (Josh. 5:2-9); David's delivery of two hundred Philistine foreskins to Saul (see DAVID AND MICHAL); the trick played on the men of Shechem by the vengeful sons of Jacob (see SHECHEM AND DINAH); and (in the Apocrypha) the forcible circumcision by Mattathias and friends of all the uncircumcised boys found in Israel (1 Macc. 2:46).

CONCEPTION: "Made in Secret"

In the biblical world, conception, aside from the prerequisite sexual intercourse, was a biological mystery: "I was made in secret," says the Psalmist (139:15), "and curiously wrought." That the male must contribute was of course taken for granted. Thus Levi before conception is considered to be "yet in the loins of his father" (Heb. 7:10), and Onan is punished for deliberately spilling his semen (Gen. 38:9-10). But the ovum, as Tikva Frymer-Kensky points out, is a relatively recent discovery. Conception in the Bible is therefore viewed as miraculous, a gift from God: "children are a heritage from the Lord, and the fruit of the womb is his reward" (Ps. 127:3). Thus when her husband Boaz "went in unto" Ruth, it was "the Lord," not Boaz, who "gave her conception" (Ruth 4:13).

Just as progeny was a sign of divine favor, so barrenness was a sign of divine punishment or of the woman being forgotten by God. There was no worse fate in a patriarchal society in which a woman's main function was the bearing of children. Hence the barren Rachel's anguished cry to Jacob: "Give me children, or else I die!" Yahweh finally "remembered" Rachel, and she conceived and bore Joseph (Gen. 30:1-2,22-24). Similarly Elkanah's wife Hannah was barren, for "the Lord had shut up her womb," till God "remembered" and "visited" Hannah (after her husband again "knew" her), "so that she conceived," bearing Samuel (1 Sam. 1:1-20).

Abraham's wife Sarah (Gen. 17:15-21; 21:1-3), Isaac's wife Rebekah (Gen. 26:21), the unnamed mother of Samson (Judg. 13:2-3), the Shunammite woman who shelters Elisha (2 Kings 4:8,14-17), and John the Baptist's mother Elizabeth (Luke 1:7-24) were all barren women who conceived by the grace of God—for whom "nothing shall be impossible" (Luke 1:37)—along with a little help from their husbands. (See also VIRGIN BIRTH: "CHILD OF THE HOLY GHOST.")

Aside from Onan's coitus interruptus (Gen. 38:6-10), there is no mention in the Bible of birth control or contraception. While some plant-derived potions and other contraceptive measures were known in the ancient world, contraception would be generally inconsistent with the early Hebrew notion of family planning, which may be summed up by the modern phrase "think big." (The family of Jair, a judge whose thirty sons "rode on thirty ass colts," and that of Abdon, a judge whose seventy male offspring "rode on seventy asses," come to mind [Judg. 10:3-4; 12:13-14].) God said, "Be fruitful and multiply"— and Onan, it should be noted, paid dearly for interrupting his coitus (see ONAN AND TAMAR).

There is also no mention in the Bible of willful abortion (on miscarriage, see Ex. 21:22, and on stillbirth, Job 3:11-12), unless one so interprets two utterances by Hosea. The prophet asks Yahweh to punish unfaithful Israel with "a miscarrying womb" (9:14)—asking God, in effect, to be an abortionist. And Hosea quotes God as saying this of his wayward people: "Their infants shall be dashed to pieces, and their women with child shall be ripped up" (13:16). The prophet Jeremiah seems to wish that he himself had been somehow aborted: "Why did I come forth from the womb," he asks (20:18), "to see labor and sorrow, with my days spent in shame?"

In the Hebrew Bible a woman suffering the pangs of childbirth is a recurring metaphor or simile for God's people in times of trouble (Isa. 13:8, 21:3, 26:17, 42:14; Hos. 13:13; Mic. 4:10), with the term "a woman in travail" used six times in Jeremiah (4:31, 6:24, 13:21, 22:23, 30:6, 49:24). In contrast, the new Jerusalem, prophesies Isaiah, will give birth painlessly to her sons (66:7-8). In the Christian Bible, John of Patmos has a Messianic vision in which "a woman clothed with the sun," crying in travail, gives birth to a manchild, with Satan standing poised to devour him (Rev. 12:1-5). The Apostle Paul describes how "the whole creation groaneth and travaileth in pain" (Rom. 8:22), with the coming judgment bringing destruction for the wicked "as travail upon a woman with child" (1 Thess. 5:3), and he likens himself to a childbearing woman: "I travail in birth," Paul tells the Galatians (4:27), "until Christ be formed in you."

CONCUBINES: "Many Strange Women"

Polygyny, or having more than one wife or mate, was accepted practice among the early Hebrews, who highly valued large families. The English word concubine (from "one to lie with" in Latin) translates the Hebrew *pilegesh*, a woman bought as a slave or otherwise acquired by a man for his sexual pleasure, or to serve as a surrogate child-bearer if his wife, or one of his wives, was barren. Thus Sarah gives her handmaid Hagar to her husband Abraham (Gen. 16:1-2), and Rachel gives Bilhah, and Leah gives Zilpah, to Jacob (Gen. 30:1-5,9), for the purpose of having children. The sons of concubines could inherit equally with those of wives, unless the father chose not to recognize them. (Thus Abraham, at his wife Sarah's insistence, disinherits his firstborn son Ishmael, the offpsring of Hagar [Gen. 21:10-14]. See Richard H. Hiers on inheritance and bequest.)

A woman sold by her father into concubinage had certain rights, so to speak, under Hebrew law (Ex. 21:7-11). A dissatisfied buyer could not resell her to a foreigner; he had either to sell her back to her father, or give her to one of his own sons and treat her as a daughter-in-law. Otherwise she was free to go, with the man who had bought her unreimbursed.

Having intercourse with another man's concubine was seen as a deliberate challenge to that man's power or authority. Thus David's son Absalom, as an act of political rebellion, has sex with ten of his father's concubines "in the sight of all Israel" (2 Sam. 16:22). When the Israelite king Ishbosheth accuses Abner, his military commander, of "going into" the royal concubine Rizpah, Abner, without denying the charge, becomes so indignant over *being* charged ("Am I a dog's head of Judah?") that he switches allegiance, joining Judah's king David, with Ishbosheth soon losing his head (2 Sam. 3:7-12, 4:5-8). King Solomon has his brother Adonijah executed for having the gall to ask for the royal concubine Abishag the Shunammite in marriage (1 Kings 2:13-25).

Reuben has sex, apparently out of pure sexual desire, with his father Jacob's concubine Bilhah, for which Reuben loses his birthright as firstborn son (Gen. 35:22; 49:3-4; 1 Chron. 5:1).

One of the grimmest passages in the Bible involves the rape of a visitor's concubine in the town of Gibeah, an outrage that leads to the marital ostracism of the Benjaminites—with a resultant shortage of women—by the other Israelite tribes (see BENJAMIN: "A RAVENOUS WOLF").

The kings of Israel and Judah took polygyny to the extreme, with Solomon being the ultimate extremist, having three hundred wives and seven hundred concubines (1 Kings 11:3). The fact that Solomon had so many "strange women" (meaning foreign ones) led later Israelite religious leaders to frown on the practice. Thus the Deuteronomic law, promulgated during the reign of Josiah, prohibits a king from "multiplying wives" (Deut. 17:17), and Ezra and Nehemiah call upon Hebrew men to stop marrying foreign women (see EZRA: "YE HAVE TAKEN STRANGE WIVES"). By the close of Old Testament times, having multiple wives and concubines, whether foreign or domestic, was no longer kosher. (See also GENDER and MARRIAGE.)

COZBI AND ZIMRI

Encamped on the plains of Moab, the children of Israel under Moses begin "to commit whoredom with the daughters of Moab," who entice the Hebrews into Baal worship at a place called Peor (see BAALIM AND ASHTAROTH). For this the Israelites are hit by Yahweh with a plague, which is threatening to wipe them out. He has also ordered that several Hebrew leaders be impaled.

As the Israelites sit bemoaning their plight by the door of the tabernacle or tent of meeting, they behold Zimri of the tribe of Simeon come traipsing home with Cozbi, the daughter of a Midianite prince. This rubs the priest Phinehas (not to mention Yahweh) the wrong way, notwithstanding the fact that Moses himself is married to a Midianite woman. (Yahweh tells Israel in Deut. 7:1-4 not to marry foreign women, for they will turn men away from the Lord "that they may serve other gods.")

Zimri takes Cozbi into the *haqqudah* (KJV and NRSV "tent," RSV "inner room"), which prompts Phinehas to go fetch a javelin. Entering the *haqqudah*, Phinehas finds Zimri and Cozbi in a position that allows him to slay them both with one thrust of the spear. This double execution turns away God's wrath and stays the plague, which claims twenty-four thousand lives.

Translators have taken stabs in the dark at *haqqudah*, a word occurring nowhere else in the Bible. If the word refers to Zimri's tent or a room therein, the story is a cautionary tale about bringing home the wrong kind of woman. If *haqqudah* refers to the tabernacle or its inner room, making love therein is a desecration of God's sanctuary (see Lev. 15:16-18)—a stronger motive, perhaps, for the action of Phinehas, praised by Sirach as "zealous in the fear of the Lord" (45:23; see also Ps. 106:30). If *haqqudah* refers to some other tent, in particular one associated with Baal worship, the story supports the view (once widely held but now seriously questioned by scholars) that cultic sex was practiced in ancient Israel and elsewhere. (See PROSTITUTION.)   (NUMBERS 25)   ⇒ RAHAB THE HARLOT

D

DAVID AND ABIGAIL

See ABIGAIL AND DAVID.

DAVID AND BATHSHEBA

See BATHSHEBA: "I AM WITH CHILD."

DAVID AND JONATHAN

See HOMOSEXUALITY: "THAT WHICH IS UNSEEMLY."

DAVID AND MICHAL

King Saul of Israel fears that the young warrior David has become too popular for Saul's own good. When Saul learns that his daughter Michal loves David, it gives the king an idea. Saul tells David that he can marry Michal if he brings him, as vengeance against Israel's enemies, one hundred Philistine foreskins. (See CIRCUMCISION.) Saul figures, of course, that such a mission will cut short David's life. But David, perhaps seeing marriage to the king's daughter as a shortcut to the throne, brings Saul not one hundred but two hundred Philistine pre-puces. Thus Michal becomes David's first wife.

When Saul later sends men to David's house with orders to kill him, Michal, putting an idol with goat's hair in the bed as a decoy, lets David down through a window to escape. With David in hiding, Saul gives Michal to a fellow named Palti. David meanwhile takes two more wives, Abigail and Ahinoam (both of whom he must then rescue from Amalekite marauders).

Anointed king of Judah in Hebron upon Saul's death, David asks the new king of Israel, Saul's son Ishbosheth, to send Michal back to him. Ishbosheth returns her to David—with poor Palti following after her weeping, till he is ordered to turn around and go home.

David in Hebron begets six children by four more wives. (On his firstborn, see AMNON AND TAMAR.) On becoming king of Israel in Jerusalem, David takes even more wives and concubines. (See ABSALOM AND THE TEN CONCUBINES and BATHSHEBA: "I AM WITH CHILD.") In all David has twenty children by his wives and an untold number by the concubines. Yet Michal all the while remains childless.

Michal becomes disgusted when she looks out a window and sees David showing himself—"leaping and dancing" ecstati-cally, wearing only an ephod (a priestly apron)—in front of the ark of God. (The Chronicler adds a robe to David's attire.) "How glorious," Michal tells David, that the king of Israel "uncovered himself today" before handmaids in public. David replies that he can be even "more vile" than that in dancing before the Lord. Michal, we are then told, has no children "to the day of her death."

(1 SAM. 18:20-27; 25:44; 2 SAM. 3:14-16; 6:12-23; 1 CHR. 3:1-9; 15:27-29)

⇒ BATHSHEBA

DELILAH: "How Canst Thou Say, I Love You?"

See SAMSON AND DELILAH.

DINAH: "Get Me This Damsel to Wife"

See SHECHEM AND DINAH.

E

ELI AND HIS TWO SONS OF BELIAL

Eli and his sons Hophni and Phinehas are priests in the sanctuary of the Lord at Shiloh. Eli, old and virtually blind, is a righteous man, but Hophni and Phinehas are real "sons of Belial" (the biblical equivalent of s.o.b.'s). The two rascals take sacrificial meat for themselves, and have sex with the women who minister at the sanctuary door.

Eli, who can't see these goings-on for himself, is told all about them by the people. "Why do ye such things?" Eli asks the boys, "for it is no good report that I hear."

As Eli is unable to restrain them, the Lord himself takes action against Hophni and Phinehas for their "evil dealings." (This Phinehas is not to be confused, of course, with the earlier priest Phinehas who takes a dim view of sex around sanctuaries [see COZBI AND ZIMRI].) Both Hophni and Phinehas, says Yahweh, "shall die the same day." As indeed they do: the two sons of Belial (the Hebrew word *belial* means "worthlessness") are slain in battle on a day when the Philistines, in addition to inflicting a "great slaughter" on the Israelites, capture the ark of the covenant.

When Eli gets word that his sons are dead, we are not told his reaction. When he hears that the ark is lost, he falls off his seat, breaking his neck, and dies. When Phinehas's pregnant wife hears of all this—the ark is lost, Eli is dead, and the last report on Phinehas is in—she goes into labor. Dying in childbirth, she names the child Ichabod ("no glory"), saying, "The glory is departed from Israel." (1 SAM. 1:1-17; 2:12-17,22-34; 3:2; 4:11-21)

⇒ ABIGAIL AND DAVID

ELIZABETH AND ZECHARIAH

In the days of King Herod of Judea, an angel appears to the priest Zechariah. "Your prayer is heard," says the angel, "your wife Elizabeth shall bear you a son, and you shall call his name John."

Zechariah, according to the angel, is supposed to "have joy and gladness." But Zechariah is skeptical. "How shall I know this?" he asks, pointing out to the angel that he and Elizabeth, who's been barren, are old. The angel testily replies, "I am Gabriel, who stands in the presence of God." And for expressing doubt at the "good news" delivered, Zechariah, declares Gabriel, shall be unable to speak until all is accomplished.

After this vision Zechariah presumably has sex with Elizabeth, during which he has nothing to say. Elizabeth conceives, and six months later she is visited by her cousin Mary, a betrothed virgin who has just heard from Gabriel too. At the sound of Mary's greeting, Elizabeth feels the baby leap in her womb.

Mary goes home after staying three months, and Elizabeth gives birth to a son. At the eighth-day circumcision there is an argument: Elizabeth wants to name the child John, while friends and relatives want to name him after his father. Zechariah contributes nothing to the conversation until asked. He gets a writing tablet and has the last word: "His name," writes Zechariah, "is John."

Zechariah with that regains his power of speech. Filled with the Holy Ghost, he prophesies that his son John will be a prophet of the Lord, "to guide our feet to the way of peace." But John the Baptist, alas, is destined also to have trouble one day over sex and the power of speech. (See HEROD AND THE DANCE OF SALOME.) (LUKE 1:5-25,57-64)

⇒ VIRGIN BIRTH

ELKANAH AND HANNAH

See HANNAH: "GIVE THY HANDMAID A MANCHILD."

EPHRAIM: "Her Rulers with Shame Do Love"

Following the Hebrew invasion of Canaan, Joseph's son Ephraim and his tribe settle in the central highlands. The Chronicler recounts an episode in which two of Ephraim's many sons are killed by the Canaanite men of Gath, who object to Ephraim's boys rustling their livestock. This plunges Ephraim into prolonged mourning, after which, we are told, he "went in to his wife." She conceives and bears a son whom Ephraim names Beriah ("misery"), "because it went evil with (Ephraim's) house."

This evil is temporary, however, as Ephraim eventually becomes a preeminent tribe of Israel. Under the Israelite monarchy the tribe's importance is such that the prophet Hosea often refers to Israel itself as Ephraim in describing its unfaithfulness to the Hebrew God Yahweh. Ephraim, says Hosea, has committed "whoredom continually," being "joined to idols," and it's not just the Ephraimite riffraff, for "her rulers with shame do love." For such conduct Hosea asks God to make Ephraim unable to bear or nurse children. Through Hosea the Lord pronounces judgment, foreshadowing the Israelite kingdom's destruction: Ephraim "shall bear no fruit: yea, though they bring forth, yet will I slay even the beloved fruit of their womb." (1 CHR. 7:20-23; HOS. 4:17-9:16)

ESTHER: "The Maiden Who Pleases the King"

In the book of Esther, King Ahasuerus (Xerxes I) of Persia, his heart "merry with wine" at a palace feast, orders that Queen

Vashti, who is holding a separate feast for the women, come and present herself. The king wants to show her off, for she is "beautiful to look at." But Vashti refuses to appear, infuriating Ahasuerus, who asks his wise men what action to take.

Vashti must go, they say, lest women everywhere follow her example and start disobeying their husbands. "Let fair young virgins be sought for the king," the wise men advise; let them be brought to the eunuch Hegai, in charge of the royal harem, and be given their cosmetics; and "let the maiden who pleases the king be queen instead of Vashti."

Ahasuerus so decrees. Of the many virgins brought to the palace and placed in Hegai's care, one is a "fair and beautiful" Jew (a person from Judah or, in the Greek-Latin form, Judea, under Persia following the Babylonian exile). She is Esther, the adopted daughter of her cousin Mordecai. The eunuch Hegai is so pleased with Esther—who, we are told, does not disclose she's a Jew, though no reason for this is stated—that he gives her the best living quarters in the harem and assigns seven maidens to serve her.

Esther and the other virgins undergo twelve months of beautification. Each virgin is then taken to spend a night with the king. Each is afterwards placed in the custody of the eunuch Shaasgaz, keeper of the king's concubines. Each will not be called in again unless Ahasuerus has "delighted in her."

When Esther's turn comes to spend the night with the king, Hegai gives her some advice, presumably about the king's sexual preferences. She is taken in to Ahasuerus, and the king delights in her indeed, loving Esther above all the others. Ahasuerus thus crowns Esther queen, replacing Vashti.

Queen Esther later learns of a plot by Haman, the king's top official, to destroy all the Jews because Mordecai won't bow down to him. Esther informs King Ahasuerus of this plot (and of the fact that she herself is a Jew) in Haman's presence. Beside himself with rage, Ahasuerus goes out into the palace garden. Haman, fearfully pleading for his life, falls down beside Esther on the couch—an act that the king misinterprets as he returns to the room: "Will he even rape the queen, right in front of me here in my house?"

Ahasuerus has Haman "hanged" (perhaps meaning impaled), on the same "gallows" (stake?) on which Haman had meant to execute Mordecai. Esther's deliverance of her people is annually commemorated by the Jewish festival of Purim. As for the vanquished Vashti, her reasons for disobeying the king are not actually stated in the story. The king's desire that she be displayed before his male guests "with the crown royal" suggests that she is expected to have nothing else on. Vashti is in any case seen by modern feminists as an admirable and tragic figure—a woman who, in Gary David Comstock's words, "gets trashed for being strong." (ESTHER) ⇒ EZRA

EUNUCHS: "Let Him Accept It Who Can"

Castrated men held positions of trust, particularly with respect to harems, in courts of the ancient Near East. Even if a eunuch were tempted to fool around with a royal concubine in his charge, he could not impregnate her. He could do little more than look at her, embrace her, and groan (Sirach 30:20).

Several eunuchs appear in the Bible. In the book of Esther, there is a division of labor: Hegai is in charge of the Persian king's incoming virgins, who upon their deflowering are looked after by Shaasgaz. In the book of Daniel, the young Daniel is shown "favour and tender love" by Ashpenaz, "the prince of the eunuchs" of Babylon's King Nebuchadnezzar (1:9). The eunuch Bagoas finds his master missing a body part in the book of Judith (14:14-15). In Israel royal eunuchs throw Jezebel from a window to her death (2 Kings 9:35), and the Ethiopian eunuch Ebedmelech helps hoist Jeremiah out of a dungeon (Jer. 38:7-13). Another castrated Ethiopian is baptized by Philip in Acts 8:27-39.

Among the Hebrews being a eunuch was not a coveted position. Thus the prophet Isaiah warns King Hezekiah that his sons "shall be eunuchs in the palace of the king of Babylon" (2 Kings 20:18). Being physically blemished, eunuchs could not serve in the Israelite priesthood (Lev. 21:20; Deut. 23:1). Still, the eunuch should not consider himself "a dry tree," says Isaiah, for God will give righteous eunuchs "an everlasting name," one "that shall not be cut off" (56:3,5). Castration is even held out to have its spiritual rewards. Thus Jesus speaks of "eunuchs for the kingdom of heaven's sake," adding "Let him accept it who can" (Matt. 19:12).

Presumably Jesus' saying, which historically is one justification for celibacy in the Catholic priesthood, is meant to encourage sexual abstinence, not literal castration. The early Christians did not have some organized equivalent of the *galli*, priests in Rome who in religious frenzy emasculated themselves in worship of Attis, the dying and reviving consort of the mother goddess Cybele (see Frazer's *The New Golden Bough*). As noted by Tom Horner, however, there were early Christians who indeed castrated themselves—the church father Origen among them—in taking literally Christ's words. The Apostle Paul, incidentally, in his letter to the Galatians (5:12), wishes that those who preach that circumcision is necessary for salvation would "cut themselves off." By that Paul could mean either castration or penile amputation—not a charitable wish either way.

EVE: "She Shall Be Called Woman"

See ADAM AND EVE *and* GENDER: "MALE AND FEMALE CREATED HE THEM."

EZEKIEL: Talking Lewd Women

Chapters 16 and 23 of the book of Ezekiel contain perhaps the most striking sexual imagery—symbolizing Israelite idolatry as well as alliances with foreign powers—to be found anywhere in ancient literature.

In chapter 16 the Hebrew God Yahweh speaks to the city of Jerusalem, portraying her as a Canaanite baby abandoned at birth, who grows up—"thy breasts are fashioned, and thine (pubic) hair is grown"—to marry Yahweh, but who becomes an insatiable adulteress. "When I passed by thee, and looked upon thee," says Yahweh, "thy time was the time of love; and I spread my skirt over thee, . . . and entered into a covenant with thee, . . . and thou becamest mine." But then "thou playedst the harlot," Yahweh accuses, "and hast opened thy feet to every one that passed by." She "committed fornication with the Egyptians," and "played the whore also with the Assyrians," even extended her fornication "unto Chaldea"—and not as a prostitute, who is hired for her services, for instead it's her lovers who are hired by Jerusalem. "Wherefore, O harlot," says the Lord, "I will gather thy lovers . . . and will (uncover) thy nakedness" before them, and "they shall stone thee with stones."

But Ezekiel—a priest and prophet ministering to the Babylonian exiles in the sixth century B.C.E.—is just warming up, as in chapter 23 he tells the allegorical story of two sisters named Oholah and Oholibah. The older of these "lewd women" was Oholah ("she of the tent"), symbolizing Samaria (the capital city of Israel), and the younger was Oholibah ("my tent is in her"), representing Jerusalem, capital of the kingdom of Judah. They both were wives of Yahweh and bore children, then became adulteresses on an international scale.

In her youth Oholah had lain with Egyptians, who "bruised the breasts of her virginity, and poured their whoredom upon her." Now she was Yahweh's, but "played the harlot" with the Assyrians, "all of them desirable young men," upon whom she doted, defiling herself with their idols. For this flagrant adultery Yahweh "delivered her into the hands of her lovers" the Assyrians, who "slew her with the sword." (Samaria fell to the Assyrians in 722 B.C.E.)

Yet her sister Oholibah, on seeing this, was even more corrupt than Oholah. She not only "doted upon the Assyrians," but was so taken by wall paintings of Babylonian men that she sent off for some. They obligingly "came to her into the bed of love, and they defiled her with their whoredom." Like her sister Oholah she had also "played the harlot in the land of Egypt," where her lovers had organs that were mulelike in size, with issue "like the issue of horses." Now she entertained drunken groups from the desert, all manner of "men of the common sort" who "went in unto" Oholah and Oholibah.

"I will raise up thy lovers against thee," the Lord tells Oholibah, and "they shall deal with thee hatefully." They will cut off her nose and ears, stone her, slay her children, and burn down her house. "Thus will I cause lewdness to cease out of the land," says Yahweh, "that all women may be taught not to do after your lewdness." Stern judgment indeed, and Ezekiel's lewd women would in any case be a tough act to follow.

(EZEKIEL 16, 23)   ⇒ SUSANNA AND THE ELDERS

EZRA: "Ye Have Taken Strange Wives"

The Jewish priest Ezra, armed with "the wisdom of (the Hebrew) God" in the form of a new codification of Mosaic law, journeys from Babylon to Judea in 398 B.C.E. ("the seventh year" of King Artaxerxes II of Persia). Ezra and his fellow travelers have been preceded by many Jews, allowed by the Persians, conquerors of Babylon in 538 B.C.E., to return to their homeland from exile. As Ezra arrives at Jerusalem, the temple is already rebuilt, and Nehemiah, the Persian-appointed governor of Judea, has rebuilt Jerusalem's walls.

But Ezra finds something that appalls him. The returned exiles have been marrying foreign women, daughters of Gentiles living in Palestine. Did not Moses say, "Neither shalt thou make marriages with (the inhabitants of the land)" (Deut. 7:3)? Yet here are Jews—even priests and other leaders of God's chosen people—marrying and having children, mingling the "holy seed" (Ezra 9:2), with the non-Jewish population.

This so upsets Ezra that he literally tears out his hair (Ezra

9:3). "O my God, I am ashamed and blush," Ezra prays, "to lift up my face to thee" (9:6). The governor Nehemiah is also upset, but he tears out other people's hair instead of his own (Neh. 13:25). Nehemiah curses and beats them, angrily asking them, "Did not Solomon king of Israel sin by these things?" (See SOLOMON AND HIS "OUTLANDISH WOMEN.") Now half of the children running around town, Nehemiah complains, can't even speak Hebrew (13:24).

A group of repentant Jews comes to Ezra while he is weeping and "casting himself down" in front of the temple. "We have trespassed against our God," group spokesman Shechaniah tells Ezra, "and have taken strange wives of the people of the land." But still "there is hope in Israel," says Shechaniah: "let us make a covenant with our God to put away all the wives, and such as are born of them." He tells Ezra to get up and take charge of the matter: "be of good courage, and do it."

Ezra gets up, and a proclamation goes out for all Jewish men to gather at Jerusalem. All the men come and sit in the street by the temple, where they tremble "because of this matter," and because it is pouring down rain where they sit.

"Ye have transgressed, and have taken strange wives," Ezra tells them, "to increase the trespass of Israel." He tells them to separate themselves "from the people of the land, and from the strange wives," and in one voice the congregation replies, "As thou hast said, so must we do." The men ask, however, that they not have to stand in line to get their divorces, "for we are many that have transgressed in this thing," and "it is a time of much rain."

Ezra obligingly selects some heads of families to handle the procedure, by which the men get their divorces by appointment, with a ram from each man as a guilt offering. As for the governor, Nehemiah congratulates himself for all this: "Thus cleansed I them of all strangers," he writes in his memoir, ending with, "Remember me, O my God, for good." (See also MARRIAGE: "THEY SHALL BE ONE FLESH.")

(EZRA 7:1-28; 9:1-10:44; NEH. 13:23-30)   ⇒ JUDITH AND HOLOFERNES

F

FLESH: "To Be Carnally Minded Is Death"

The Hebrew word *bashar* can refer to the flesh of one's body, to the body as a whole, to one's kin, or to all living creatures. It can also refer to the penis, as in Abraham being "circumcised in the flesh" (Gen. 17:11,14,24), a man having an "issue out of his flesh" (Lev. 15:2), and the Egyptian lovers of the whore Oholibah having members like "the flesh of asses" (Ezek. 23:20).

In the New Testament the Apostle Paul, reflecting an ascetic dualism of body and spirit found in Greco-Roman philosophy, associates flesh (Greek *sarkos*) with animalistic urges or sinfulness. "To be carnally minded is death," says Paul, whereas "to be spiritually minded is life and peace" (Rom. 7:14; 8:6). Topping Paul's list of manifest "works of the flesh" are adultery and fornication (Gal. 5:19). "If ye live after the flesh, ye shall die," Paul writes to the Romans (8:13), "but if ye through the Spirit do mortify the deeds of the body, ye shall live." Thus Paul tells them to "make not provision for the flesh, to fulfill the lusts thereof" (13:14). Similarly the First Letter of Peter urges the faithful to "abstain from fleshly lusts, which war against the soul" (1 Pet. 2:11), and the Second Letter condemns false teachers, who as "natural brute beasts," with "eyes full of adultery," allure "unstable souls" by "the lusts of the flesh, through much wantonness" (2 Pet. 2.12-18).

FORNICATION: "Going after Strange Flesh"

In English translations of the Old Testament, "fornication" and
"playing the harlot" are terms used to translate the Hebrew
zenut (verb form *zanah*), connoting sexual intercourse outside
of marriage. Such conduct is used metaphorically to refer to
Hebrew idolatry. In the New Testament, "fornication" translates the Greek word *porneia* ("harlotry" or "prostitution"),
which Paul and others use broadly to include any illicit sexual
activity. Thus adultery, bestiality, homosexuality, incest, and
rape, against all of which there are scriptural laws, are biblically
acts of fornication, or, to borrow a phrase from the Letter of
Jude (1:7), "going after strange flesh."

There is more fornication in Ezekiel 23, a lurid allegory of
Hebrew apostasy, than in any other chapter in the Bible. Coming in a close second is Ezekiel 16, an allegory of adulterous
Jerusalem. Indeed Ezekiel on illicit sex is almost in a class by
himself (see EZEKIEL: TALKING LEWD WOMEN), though
certainly the other Old Testament prophets as a group have
plenty to say (and in the case of Hosea, to do) on the subject
(virtually always as a metaphor of Israel's unfaithfulness to
Yahweh; see HARLOTRY: "A-WHORING AFTER OTHER
GODS"; JEREMIAH: "THY LOVERS WILL DESPISE THEE";
and HOSEA: "UPON EVERY CORNFLOOR").

In the New Testament's book of Revelation, John of
Patmos portrays imperial Rome (called "Babylon") as "the
great whore" and "mother of harlots," with whom "the kings of
the earth have commited fornication" (17:1-5). John also complains in Rev. 2:20-23 about an individual in Thyatira, a
"Jezebel" and self-styled prophetess who seduces the faithful
"to commit fornication." For her lack of repentance, John
threatens to "cast her into a (sick) bed" and "kill her children
with death."

The Apostle Paul, in his first letter to the Corinthians, tells
the faithful to "flee fornication" (6:18), to "let every man have
his own wife" and "every woman have her own husband" (if one

is compelled to by desire, it being the ascetic Paul's preference, in view of the impending end of the world, that Christians stay single and celibate, focused on the glory to come [7:1-8,32-33]). Paul reminds them that fornicators are not among those who will "inherit the kingdom of God" (6:9-10).

The Letter of Jude is more direct about punishment: like the cities of Sodom and Gomorrah, those guilty of fornication will suffer "the vengeance of eternal fire" (1:7).

The Apocalypse of Peter, a noncanonical work dating probably from the early second century (see Barnstone's *The Other Bible*), describes how fornicators are hung over a burning pit in hell, the women by their necks and plaited hair and the men by their genitals. The men complain among themselves that they didn't know this was coming.

G

GENDER: "Male and Female Created He Them"

Ancient Israel, like other nations of the ancient Near East, was a patriarchal society, meaning that it was centered around the fathers of families, with descent and inheritance being patrilineal or through the male line. (A daughter could inherit property from a father who had no son, but she had to marry within her father's tribe: see Num. 27:1-8 and 36:6-12 on the daughters of Zelophehad.)

Women in this society had subordinate status and were under the sexual control of men. Thus a daughter was to stay a virgin till married off (she could be stoned to death if she didn't), earning her father a *mohar* or bride price from the bridegroom's family. Once married, the woman's principal role was that of childbearing. She was considered for all practical purposes to be the property of her husband (Hebrew *baal*, "lord" or "master"), who was free to have more than one wife—monogamy was the ideal, but there was no set limit—all the more to obey the divine commandment to "be fruitful and multiply" (Gen. 1:28).

By New Testament times, a Jewish man was usually the lord or master of only one wife at a time. But the image of woman suffered from the stress that postexilic priests placed on ritual purity, which, to quote Léonie J. Archer, made women, due to the blood of menstruation and childbirth, "unclean for a large part of their lives." Hellenistic Jewish writers began expressing the same contempt for women that made the views of the Greeks on gender, in Giulia Sissa's words, "distinctly unpalatable." Thus the Jewish philosopher Philo (first century C.E.) identifies man with mind and reason, and woman with irrationality and the senses. "A silent wife," says the apocryphal Sirach (second century B.C.E.), "is a gift from the Lord" (26:14). The Jewish historian Josephus, a contemporary of Philo, puts it succinctly: "Women are inferior to men in every way" (*Against Apion* II:201).

The behavior of Jesus Christ toward women—he included them among his disciples (Matt. 27:55-56; Mark 15:40-41; Luke 8:2-3), spoke indiscriminately to women in public (John 4:5-27), and in general treated females as if they were equal to males— was scandalously unconventional. In the Apostle Paul's day women were among leaders of the early Christian community (see Fiorenza's *In Memory of Her*, and Newsom and Ringe's *The Women's Bible Commentary*), but leadership roles for women in the church died soon after Paul did. (See PAUL.)The Apostle, though saying there is "neither male nor female," for all are "one in Christ Jesus" (Gal. 3:28), ironically set a standard for the misogyny that would become institutionalized in the church after him, and that would return all women to subordinate status, with his statement (not actually his—Paul is reading the Corinthians' words back to them), "It is good for a man not to touch a woman" (1 Cor. 7:1). Convinced that the world was soon coming to an end, Paul preferred that men and women forget about marriage and its hassles, and thus sexually abstain. (Procreation, in the world's last days, was naturally no longer a concern.) The Apostle nonetheless felt that those who could not contain their desire should marry (1 Cor. 7:9), and that husbands and wives, for fidelity's sake, should have sex on a regular basis (1 Cor. 7:2-5).

What Fiorenza calls the post-Pauline "patriarchalization" of the church is reflected in the subordination of women that is required in the First Letter to Timothy (purportedly written by Paul but, most scholars agree, based on content and style, composed after Paul's death): "Let the woman learn in silence with all subjection. But I suffer not a woman to teach, nor to usurp authority over the man, but to be in silence" (2:11-12).

(Also suspected by scholars to be a later non-Pauline insertion in the First Letter to the Corinthians is the command, "Let your women keep silence in the churches" [1 Cor. 14:34].)

But such subjection, it appears, was not something originally meant to exist between the sexes. According to Hebrew legend, the first woman God created as a companion for the first man Adam was a strong-willed lady named Lilith. (See Graves and Patai's *Hebrew Myths* and Reuther's *Womanguides*.) As both had been created from dust, Lilith considered herself equal to Adam. (They differed anatomically, of course, with the Bible referring to a male as one who "pisseth against the wall" [1 Sam. 25:34; 1 Kings 14:10; 21:21].) Lilith objected to having to lie beneath Adam during sexual intercourse, but Adam would have it no other way. Lilith up and left him, winding up in rabbinic tradition as a baby-killing demoness who seduces sleeping men. Lilith is mentioned in Isa. 34:14, though the KJV renders *lilith* as "screech owl." This first wife of Adam may safely be called the world's first uppity woman.

With Lilith departed, Adam was back where he started, being without a fit helper. According to a Hebrew tradition cited in Graves and Patai, God let Adam watch while he put a second woman together. The process of anatomical assemblage was so disgusting that Adam found the woman repulsive even though she was beautiful when finished. God sent this first Eve away and tried again: while Adam slept, Yahweh created the Eve found in Genesis 2 from Adam's rib. God presented her to Adam, who said happily, "This is now bone of my bones, and flesh of my flesh: she shall be called Woman, because she was taken out of Man" (Gen. 2:23).

Being "taken out of Man" need not imply a subordinate role, but rather, as Adam's rhapsodizing words suggest, a one-ness of flesh. Phyllis Trible points out that the Hebrew word *ezer* is mistranslated "helper," as the word rather connotes "companion," an equal partner. Such equality is more explicit in the first Genesis creation account (1:26-27), in which man and woman are created simultaneously ("male and female created he them"). Indeed the Bible makes clear that the subordination of women is the result of the first couple's disobedience (the eating of forbidden fruit): Yahweh tells Eve that, as part of her share of divine punishment, "thy desire shall be to thy husband, and he shall rule over thee" (3:16). Thus the Bible's patriarchal social system, far from being presented as an ideal, is seen as the result of a fall from grace.

The Christian church, influenced by the same Hellenistic misogyny that helped inspire Josephus, Philo, and such pseudepigraphical works as the Testament of Reuben ("For women are evil, my children" [5:1]; see Kee), would blame the Fall on Eve: "Adam was not deceived, but the woman being deceived was in the transgression" (1 Tim. 2:14). ("She gave me of the tree," Adam whines to God, "and I did eat" [Gen. 3:13]. Thus Adam defends himself, notes William E. Phipps, by complaining about "having to eat what his wife served him.") Yet woman can still be saved, the First Letter to Timothy allows, by having man's babies: "she shall be saved in childbearing," as long as she also has "faith and charity" and stays sober (2:15).

Can egalitarian grace be restored? Not in this world, if we are to judge by the pronouncements of Paul, whether Paul actually pronounced them or not. According to Christ, such a blissful time ultimately will come: in the hereafter ("the resurrection"), says Jesus in Luke 20:34-36, there will be no marriages, for men and women alike will be "equal unto the angels." But that's little comfort to feminist women, who would like to have equality with mere mortal men this side of eternity. (See also MARRIAGE: "THEY SHALL BE ONE FLESH.")

GENITALS: "They Knew that They Were Naked"

The Hebrews, true to Yahweh's commandment to "be fruitful and multiply" (Gen. 1:28), placed a high priority on progeny. "I will multiply your seed," Yahweh told Abraham, "as the stars of heaven and as the sand on the seashore" (Gen. 22:17). It was Abraham and his seed, of course, who had to do all the actual multiplying. The genitals, as seat of the powers of procreation, accordingly had a sacrosanct quality. Men would literally swear by them: one man might place his hand on or near another man's privates when swearing something to him, as a person today might place a hand on a Bible. (The dying Jacob, in getting Joseph to promise to "bury me not" in Egypt, tells him first, "Put, I pray thee, thy hand under my thigh" (Gen. 47:29; see also 24:2-3).

The genitals of Israelite priests had to be unblemished; under the ritual purity system, God could not be served by a eunuch or by anyone with his "stones broken" or with a missing "privy member" (Lev. 21:20; Deut. 23:1). And any woman who tried to help her husband in a fight by grabbing a combatant by the genitals was to have her hand cut off—a hands-off policy found in Deut. 25:11-12.

A biblical term frequently used for illicit sexual activity is "to uncover the nakedness" of the person whose genitals or nakedness (Hebrew *erwa*) one should not be uncovering (Lev. 18:6-16; 20:11-21). Ever since Adam and Eve, it was also shameful for a person's genitals to be exposed in public. (When Adam and Eve, blissfully unclothed in Eden, sinned against God through disobedience, they immediately reacted with a new-found shame: "They knew that they were naked" [Gen. 3:6-7].) Thus the king of Ammon subjects David's servants to public humiliation by shaving them and cutting off their garments "hard by their buttocks" (1 Chr. 19:4). The prophet Isaiah—who incidentally walked around naked for three years as a bad sign to Egypt and Ethiopia (Isa. 20:3)—warns King Ahaz of Israel that the Assyrians will shave off the Israelites' pubic hair (7:20) (literally "hair of the feet," feet being a euphemism for genitalia [see also Ex. 4:25 and Ruth 3:7]), and later tells the "virgin daughter of Babylon" to "make bare the leg, uncover the thigh," for "thy nakedness shall be uncovered, yea, thy shame shall be seen" (47:1-3). Judahites captured by Assyria, says Micah, are to be led away with their "shame naked" (1:11). Jeremiah quotes Yahweh as telling whorish Jerusalem that he will lift her skirts over her face and expose her genitals (13:26), and in Nahum the "harlot" Nineveh is told the same ((3:5). Likewise in Ezekiel God tells Jerusalem that he will gather all her lovers around her and uncover her nakedness before them (16:37).

Priests had to wear linen breeches lest their unblemished genitals be glimpsed—apparently from the vantage-point of the floor—during services (Ex. 28:42-43). There was nothing wrong, on the other hand, with prophets stripping and dancing around naked during religious ecstasy, or, as mentioned, simply walking around naked as a sign. ("I will wail and howl," says Micah [1:8], "I will go stripped and naked.") Even King Saul once stripped and "prophesied" when the "Spirit of God" came upon him (1 Sam. 19:23-24). It was probably in a similar ecstasy that King David danced publicly before the ark clad only in a priestly apron (2 Sam. 6:12-16). When his disgusted wife Michal complained of this spectacle, David retaliated by apparently denying her his nakedness for the rest of her childless life (see DAVID AND MICHAL).

GIBEAH AND THE LEVITE'S CONCUBINE

See BENJAMIN: "A RAVENOUS WOLF."

GIDEON: Seventy Sons plus One

In the time of the judges, the people of Israel offer to crown as king a farmer named Gideon, after he leads them to victory over invading Midianites. Gideon has also helped turn his people away from the cult of the Canaanite fertility god Baal and goddess Asherah.

Gideon turns down the offer of kingship to concentrate on raising a family. He does ask all the men of Israel to give him their golden earrings. which they do. With the earrings Gideon makes a fancy ephod (a priestly garment, here perhaps clothing an idol), which he puts in his hometown of Ophrah, and which

the Israelites promptly start worshipping ("all Israel went thither
a-whoring after it"). (See also AARON AND THE GOLDEN
CALF.) How long this goes on is not stated, though it is "a snare"
to Gideon and his family.

As for the family, seventy sons, we are told, are "of his body
begotten," for Gideon has "many wives. " To top things off, a
concubine of Gideon in Shechem bears Abimelech, son number
seventy-one.

Gideon dies "in a good old age," immediately after which
the people again go "a-whoring after Baalim." The concubine's
son Abimelech kills all but one of his seventy half-brothers (the
youngest, Jotham, escapes) and has himself crowned king in
Shechem. His reign is shortlived, however, as Abimelech gets
crowned by a woman with a millstone while attacking Thebez.
Mortally wounded, Abimelech has his armorbearer kill him,
"that men say not of me, A woman slew him."   (JUDG. 8:22-9:57)

⇒ SAMSON AND DELILAH

GOD/LORD/YAHWEH

See YAHWEH: "THY MAKER IS THINE HUSBAND."

GOLDEN CALF, WORSHIP OF THE

See AARON AND THE GOLDEN CALF.

GOMER THE WHORE

See HOSEA: "UPON EVERY CORNFLOOR."

H

HAGAR THE HANDMAID

See ABRAHAM AND SARAH.

HAM AND THE CURSE OF CANAAN

See NOAH: UNSUNK, AND DRUNK AS A SKUNK.

HANNAH: "Give Thy Handmaid a Manchild"

An Ephraimite named Elkanah has two wives. One, Penninah, bears him several sons and daughters, but Hannah (Hebrew "grace") remains childless, for Yahweh has "shut up her womb." The fertile Penninah taunts her to tears, but Elkanah loves Hannah, saying, "Why weepest thou? . . . Am I not better to thee than ten sons?"

When the family goes to worship in Shiloh, Hannah prays "in bitterness of soul" in the Lord's sanctuary. She asks Yahweh to "remember" her, and makes God a vow: "Give thy handmaid a manchild, and I will give him to thee, Lord, all the days of his life," and no razor shall ever touch his head—meaning he will be consecrated as a Nazirite (see SAMSON AND DELILAH).

Eli the priest, sitting by a post in the sanctuary, is watching Hannah tearfully pray, her lips silently moving. Old and nearly blind, Eli misinterprets this behavior. He reproaches Hannah for drinking too much.

Hannah responds that she is not "a daughter of Belial" (that is, a worthless woman) but rather is of "sorrowful spirit," that she has not drunk anything but has "poured out" her soul to the Lord. To this Eli replies, "Go in peace, and the God of Israel grant thee thy petition."

This lifts Hannah's spirits. Upon their return home, Elkanah, we are told, "knew Hannah his wife, and the Lord remembered her." Hannah conceives and bears a manchild named Samuel.

When the child is weaned, Hannah takes him to Eli, to dedicate him to the Lord's service as promised. "I have lent him to the Lord," Hannah says. Eli thanks her for "the loan," saying, "The Lord give thee seed" in return. And indeed "the Lord," so her story concludes, "visited Hannah, so that she conceived, and bare three sons and two daughters." As for Samuel, he grows up to be a prophet, anointing Saul as the first king of Israel.

(1 SAM. 1:1-28; 2:20-21)   ⇒ ELI AND HIS TWO SONS OF BELIAL

HARLOTRY: "A-Whoring after Other Gods"

A harlot (*zonah*) in ancient Israel was a person to be avoided, according to scripture, for both economic and moral reasons, though prostitution was not illegal (provided the woman was single, that is, not committing adultery, and not a priest's daughter, "profaning her father" [Lev. 21:9]). Thus the Hebrew Bible warns that consorting with prostitutes (*zanah* being the verb form for sexual intercourse outside of marriage) can leave one broke ("He that keepeth company with harlots spendeth his substance" [Prov. 29:3]), and the Apocrypha states that right abhors wrong "just as a respectable and virtuous woman abhors a harlot" (2 Esdras 16:49-50). In Jesus's parable of the Prodigal Son, a young man's whoring leads to his ruin (Luke 15:11-32), and the Apostle Paul says that a man who is "joined to an harlot" becomes "one body" with her, thus profaning that which belongs to the Lord (1 Cor. 6:13-16). Not surprisingly, "whoremongers" are among those who "shall have their part," says the book of Revelation, in the lake of fire and brimstone (21:8; see also Eph. 5:5 and Heb. 13:4; for more on hell and sex, see FORNICATION: "GOING AFTER STRANGE FLESH").

Harlotry or whoredom (*zenut*) is often used in the Old Testament as a metaphor for the recurring idolatry of the Hebrew people. Thus they are described as "playing the harlot" (Ezek. 16:41) and "a-whoring after other gods" such as Baal of Canaan (Ex. 34:15-16; Judg. 2:17, 8:33; see BAALIM AND ASHTAROTH). The prophet Jeremiah accuses "backsliding Israel" of playing the harlot "upon every high mountain and under every green tree," followed by "her treacherous sister Judah" (3:6-8). The prophet Hosea, decrying "the spirit of whoredoms" that leads Israel to seek counsel from idols (4:12), even marries a whore, to personify how Israel "hath committed great whoredom, departing from the Lord" (1:2; see HOSEA: "UPON EVERY CORNFLOOR"). (For the long-held view, now seriously questioned, that such biblical passages are not all metaphorical but include references to fertility rites or cultic sex, see PROSTITUTION: IS NOTHING SACRED?)

Wicked cities, Hebrew and non-Hebrew, are also referred to as harlots. Ezekiel 23 describes the profligacy of the sisters Oholah and Oholibah, symbolizing Samaria and Jerusalem, in language that is not used in church (see EZEKIEL: TALKING LEWD WOMEN); the prophet Nahum condemns "the whoredoms of the well-favoured harlot" Nineveh (3:2); Isaiah describes Tyre as a whore who fornicates internationally (23:15-17); and Revelation depicts imperial Rome ("Babylon") as "the great whore" and "the mother of harlots" (17:1,5).

Still, idolatry and wicked cities aside, the moral judgments of society did not prevent some "respectable" men in the Bible, as in all historical ages, from enjoying the services of harlots. The Hebrew judge Samson may have done more whoring than judging (Judg. 16:1-4), and Jacob's son Judah, mistaking his own veiled daughter-in-law for a roadside harlot, immediately hired her (Gen. 38:13-18). The tribal leader Gilead fathered Jephthah by a harlot—as a result of which Jephthah's half-brothers, upon dividing the family inheritance, conveniently left Jephthah out (Judg. 11:1-2).

A Canaanite harlot named Rahab became a heroine of the Hebrew conquest and the mother of Ruth's husband Boaz (Josh. 2:1-21; 6:17,21-25; Matt. 1:5). King Solomon, in a famous case used to illustrate his wisdom, handled a dispute between two harlots who claimed the same child (1 Kings 3:16-28). And Jesus makes the point that harlots who believed John the Baptist will enter the kingdom of God before the chief priests and elders who rejected John's message (Matt. 21:31-32). Typically, though, the Bible, reflecting a patriarchal society, is more concerned with harlotry's victimization of males than with the fate of the harlots themselves. "She sitteth at the door of her house," says Proverbs (9:14-18), to call passersby, and let him who "is simple," who "wanteth understanding," "turn in hither," for "he knoweth not that the dead are there," that "her guests are in the depths of hell." (See also EPHRAIM: "HER RULERS WITH SHAME DO LOVE" and ISRAEL: "BEGET SONS AND DAUGHTERS.")

HEROD AND THE DANCE OF SALOME

When ascetic, camel hair-clad John the Baptist appears in the Judean wilderness preaching "a baptism of repentance for the forgiveness of sins," even Herod Antipas, the tetrarch (governor) of Galilee, considers him "a righteous and holy man." This opinion is not shared by Herod's wife Herodias, however, when John attacks their incestuous marriage. "It is not lawful," John tells Herod, "for thee to have thy brother's wife" (see INCEST: "COME LIE WITH ME, MY SISTER").

Herodias is not only Herod's sister-in-law but his niece. Even the gospel writers get confused by this family, as

Herodias's previous husband, according to the Jewish historian Josephus, was not Herod's brother and fellow Palestinian tetrarch Philip (as biblically stated), but another of Herod's brothers in Rome. It is Salome, Herodias's daughter from that incestuous marriage, who eventually marries Philip, both Salome's and her mother's uncle.

The "perplexed" Herod has John imprisoned, not so much to punish him as to protect him from Herodias, who wants "to kill him." But then, at a birthday banquet for Herod, young Salome dances for her stepfather and his guests. The only gospel description of the dance is that it "pleased Herod," but Herod's words of appreciation suggest a remarkable performance indeed. "Ask me for whatever you wish, and I will grant it," Herod tells Salome. "Whatever you ask for I will give you, even half of my kingdom."

Salome consults with her mother Herodias, who tells her to ask for the head of John the Baptist on a platter. Salome duly makes the request, and Herod, not wanting to renege on a promise before his guests, reluctantly gives the order. John's head, we are told, "was brought on a platter and given to the girl, and she brought it to her mother." Thus the story of Salome's dance—what Richard Mühlberger has appropriately called "the only truly sensual episode in the New Testament"— comes to a macabre conclusion. (MATT. 14:1-12; MARK 6:16-28)

⇒ JESUS CHRIST

HOLOFERNES AND JUDITH

See JUDITH AND HOLOFERNES.

HOMOSEXUALITY: "That Which Is Unseemly"

"Thou shalt not lie with mankind, as with womankind," says Lev. 18:22, for "it is abomination." Lying with womankind—that is, reproducing—was the first of God's laws ("Be fruitful and multiply" [Gen. 2:28]), and what probably made homosexuality among the Hebrews abominable was the fact that it was no way to go about reproducing. It was a waste of seed and contrary to the created order of things, God having made man "male and female" (Gen. 1:27)—"Adam and Eve," as someone has said, "not Adam and Steve"—that they might propagate as commanded.

The book of Leviticus later specifies the penalty for homosexual lovers: if a man lies "with mankind, as he lieth with a woman," both men "shall surely be put to death; their blood shall be upon them" (20:13).

In the New Testament, the Apostle Paul includes homosexuality under what he terms "vile affections": he deplores men "leaving the natural use of the woman," lusting instead for one another, "men with men working that which is unseemly" (Rom. 1:24-27). In the same passage Paul also attacks women lying with women, in the only reference to lesbian activity in the Bible. (See LESBIANISM: "AGAINST NATURE.")

The Bible's view of homosexuality thus appears to be unequivocally negative. Little wonder that there are no homosexual biblical characters—at least none who are "out." (On the apparent exception of the men of Sodom and Gibeah, see SODOM[Y] AND GOMORRAH.) It has been long conjectured that David and King Saul's son Jonathan were more than good buddies. We are told that there was a "covenant" between them (1 Sam. 20:8), that Jonathan "delighted much in David" (19:2), that each loved the other "as he loved his own soul" (2 Sam. 18:1, 20:17), and that during their last meeting "they kissed one another, and wept one with the other" (20:41). On the death of his "brother" Jonathan, David laments, "Very pleasant hast thou been unto me: thy love to me was wonderful, passing the love of women" (2 Sam. 1:26). (Since David certainly did not pass up loving women, any sexual relationship with Jonathan would mean that David was bisexual. He may have married Michal for power, Abigail perhaps for her wealth, and as an old man he was impotent with Abishag, but the attraction of

Bathsheba was hormonal.)

The Rev. John Williams, author of *Just As I Am: A Practical Guide to Being Out, Proud, and Christian*, is convinced that Jesus Christ was gay. The evidence Williams cites includes the fact that Jesus had no wife (highly unusual for a rabbi of his time), and had in his company the so-called beloved disciple, an unidentified follower in the Gospel of John whom "Jesus loved" and who "was leaning on Jesus' bosom" at the last supper (13:23). (See JESUS CHRIST.) The sexual orientation of the Apostle Paul, a celibate who attacks homosexuality but suffers from some "thorn in the flesh" (2 Cor. 12:7), has also been a subject of speculation.

But such speculations aside, how if at all, considering the death penalty set forth in Leviticus, can gay Jews and Christians find biblical support for their lifestyle? The Rev. Williams makes a wily but unconvincing attempt to wiggle out of Leviticus: he sees the commandment against lying with a man as with a woman as meaning that during sex one man should not force another "into the receptive role," thus degrading him, in the patriarchal view, by treating him like a woman. The commandment "has nothing to say," Williams claims, "about mutual, consensual queer sex." But there is a far less fanciful explanation for the awkward or wordy way in which the Old Testament describes homosexuality (that is, lying with a man as with a woman): in biblical Hebrew there was no word for homosexuality. Likewise Paul uses roundabout language—"men with men working," etc.—for lack of a word for homosexuality in biblical Greek. (The rare word *arsenokoitai* [literally "men lying with men," NRSV "sodomites"], used in 1 Cor. 6:9 and 1 Tim. 1:10, may have been coined by Hellenistic Jews from the language of Leviticus as they found it in Greek translation [see Furnish].) In any case the point seems clear in both testaments, however clumsily worded: homosexual acts were forbidden, irrespective of who played what role whether by choice or coercion.

Dr. Robert Goss, in his book *Jesus Acted Up: A Gay and Lesbian Manifesto*, uses a different tact in trying to get around Leviticus. What the Leviticus law prohibits, according to Goss,

is male cultic prostitution. But this involves, among other problems, an unfounded premise: the existence of male cultic prostitution. ("There are six references," Goss states, "to male cultic
prostitutes [*qadesh*] in the Hebrew Scriptures. " Actually there
may be none at all. See PROSTITUTION.)

The Jewish scholar Jacob Milgrom argues that the Leviticus
prohibition of homosexuality applies only to Jewish males. This
lets ninety-nine percent of the world's homosexuals off the
hook—but unfortunately, as Milgrom acknowledges, not "the
small number of male Jewish gays."

And what do gay Christians then do about the homophobia
of Paul? John Boswell's argument that Paul is not attacking
homosexuals, but only heterosexuals involved in homosexual
activity, is no more convincing than Williams's interpretation of
Leviticus. Gays would seem to have little recourse but to dismiss
Paul and turn for support to Christ, who, in Goss's words,
practiced "solidarity with oppressed men and women," which
today includes "the sexually oppressed." Thus Jesus is seen as
"gay/lesbian sensitive"—which certainly sounds better than
Goss's statement that "God is HIV-positive."

HOSEA: "Upon Every Cornfloor"

"I found Israel," says the Hebrew God Yahweh in the book of
Hosea, "like grapes in the wilderness" (9:10). But like an unfaithful wife, Israel—whom the prophet Hosea also refers to as
Ephraim (a preeminent Israelite tribe) and Samaria (Israel's
capital city)—turns to idolatry, "playing the harlot" (4:15), her
"lovers" being Baal and the other Canaanite gods (2:13). In
their adultery, says Hosea of the Israelites, they are like "an
oven heated by the baker," an oven flaming in the morning while
the drunken baker sleeps (7:4-6).

As if to symbolize his people's apostasy, Yahweh commands
Hosea to "Go, take unto thee a wife of whoredoms and children
of whoredoms, for the land hath committed great whoredom,

departing from the Lord" (1:2). Hosea accordingly marries Gomer, a whore who bears three children—Jezreel ("God sows"), Loruhamah ("Not pitied"), and Loammi ("Not my people")—who are apparently not Hosea's (1:3-9; 2:4).

Not surprisingly Gomer leaves Hosea, after which Yahweh tells the prophet, "Go yet, love a woman beloved of her friend, yet an adulteress" (3:1). This is generally thought to be Gomer again, though it may be a second woman. In any case Hosea's love for the woman despite her adultery reflects Yahweh's love for and redemption of the chastised children of Israel (2:16-20; 3:5; 5:15-6:3; 14:4-7).

Hosea dutifully buys the woman (we are not told from whom) for fifteen pieces of silver and several bushels of barley. "Thou shalt abide for me many days," Hosea tells her, "thou shalt not play the harlot, and thou shalt not be for another man" (3:1-3). But the habitually unfaithful Israel, who loves "a reward upon every cornfloor" (9:1), seems unable to abide for long. Hosea thus calls upon Yahweh to make Ephraim miscarrying and milkless (9:14), and prophesies the slaughter of children and pregnant women in Samaria (13:16). Not even the kingdom of Judah to the south will escape divine punishment: "I will pour out my wrath upon (the princes of Judah) like water" (5:10; see also 12:2).

The book of Hosea ends with hopeful words of Israel's restoration. But Hosea's imagery of violence toward women (not to mention toward children)—imagery that is continued by other prophets (see ISAIAH, JEREMIAH, and EZEKIEL)—is no less troubling to feminist commentators. "Let her therefore put away her whoredoms . . . and her adulteries from between her breasts," says Yahweh, lest "I strip her naked" and (comparing her to parched land) "slay her with thirst" (2:2-3). "And I will not have mercy on her children," he goes on, "for they be the children of whoredoms" (2:4). "(I will uncover) her lewdness in the sight of her lovers, and none," says Yahweh, "shall deliver her out of mine hand" (2:10). (See YAHWEH: "THY MAKER IS THINE HUSBAND.")   (HOSEA)   ⇒ ISAIAH

I

IDOLATRY: "Playing the Harlot"

See BAALIM AND ASHTORETH *and* HARLOTRY: "A-WHOR-ING AFTER OTHER GODS."

IMMANUEL, THE SIGN OF

See ISAIAH: "TREMBLE, YE WOMEN" *and* VIRGIN BIRTH: "CHILD OF THE HOLY GHOST."

INCEST: "Come Lie with Me, My Sister"

"None of you," says Yahweh in Lev. 18:6, "shall approach to any that is near of kin to him, to uncover their nakedness." Specifically forbidden, in the list that follows this verse, are sexual relations between a man and his mother or father's wife, sister or half-sister, granddaughter, aunt, daughter-in-law, or sister-in-law (18:7-16). (An exception is levirate marriage to one's sister-in-law; see MARRIAGE: "THEY SHALL BE ONE FLESH.") A man's daughter, not specifically mentioned, would be included with his mother and sister under "near of kin." A man is also forbidden to "vex" his wife by marrying her sister while the wife is still living (18:18).

Notable instances of incest in the Hebrew Bible are: Lot's

daughters contriving to have children by him (see LOT AND HIS DAUGHTERS); Tamar contriving to have a child by her father-in-law Judah (see JUDAH AND TAMAR); Jacob marrying Leah and Rachel, who were sisters, and Reuben having sex with his father's wife Bilhah (see JACOB AND LABAN'S DAUGH-TERS); Abraham's marriage to his half-sister Sarah (Gen. 20:12); and Amnon's rape of his half-sister Tamar (see AMNON AND TAMAR). On incest in the New Testament, see HEROD AND THE DANCE OF SALOME.

It should be noted that if Adam and Eve were the first human beings, incest, for population growth, was a practical necessity during the first few human generations (see CAIN: THE FIRST HELL EVER RAISED.) It should also be noted that all of the above cited instances of incest in the Old Testament, except for Amnon's rape of Tamar, antedate the so-called Holiness Code in Leviticus (ch. 17-26) that prohibits them. Even the rape may antedate the code in its written form.

That does not mean, of course, that Amnon telling Tamar, "Come lie with me, my sister," then forcing her to do so, is therefore to be excused. And what about the Holiness Code's author? Though the espousals are allegorical, Yahweh himself violates Lev. 18:18 by marrying two women who are sisters—and rather lewd ones at that! (See EZEKIEL: TALKING LEWD WOMEN).

INTERCOURSE, SEXUAL

See LOVEMAKING: TO KNOW IN THE BIBLICAL SENSE.

ISAAC AND REBEKAH

In his old age the Hebrew patriarch Abraham, dwelling in prosperity among the Canaanites, wishes to find a Hebrew wife

for his son Isaac, who, still single at forty, is mourning the death
of his mother. Calling in his oldest servant, Abraham tells him,
"Put, I pray thee, thy hand under my thigh." The servant does
so, in an ancient form of oath-taking (see GENITALS: "THEY
KNEW THAT THEY WERE NAKED"), and Abraham makes
him swear that he will not take a wife for Isaac from among the
daughters of Canaan. The servant promises to go instead to
Abraham's Mesopotamian homeland, to find a wife for Isaac
among Abraham's kindred.

The servant dutifully journeys to the Mesopotamian town
of Nahor, and at a well runs into just the right woman, a virgin
"fair to look upon," and a cousin of Isaac's, named Rebekah.
Her brother Laban, impressed by the gold ring and bracelets
that the servant bestows on Rebekah, invites the man to the
house. There the family, on hearing the servant describe the
great wealth that Isaac is to inherit from his father Abraham,
agrees to a marriage, and sends Rebekah off to Canaan with the
servant, with these parting words: "Thou art our sister, be thou
the mother of thousands of millions, and let thy seed possess the
gate of those which hate them."

Isaac is meditating in the field when he sees the camels
coming. When Rebekah sees Isaac, she alights from her camel,
and Isaac takes her into his late mother's tent. Rebekah "became his wife," we are told, "and he loved her: and Isaac was
comforted after his mother's death."

Rebekah is barren, but when Isaac makes entreaty of the
Lord, she conceives. She has twins who struggle within her
womb. First out is a boy with shaggy red hair, appropriately
named Esau ("hairy"); he will be a hunter and the favorite of
Isaac. The other twin is prophetically named Jacob
("supplanter"), who at birth grabs Esau by the heel. Rebekah
will be partial to Jacob.

When a famine hits the land, Isaac and Rebekah head
toward Egypt, but the Lord stops them at the Philistine town of
Gerar. (Two problems with this interlude are: no mention of
Esau and Jacob, and the fact that Philistine towns did not exist
in the days of Isaac and Rebekah.) "Sojourn in this land,"

Yahweh tells Isaac, "and I will be with thee . . . I will make thy seed to multiply as the stars of heaven, . . . and in thy seed shall all the nations of the earth be blessed."

Isaac and Rebekah stay in Gerar, but Isaac, fearing the men there might kill him to take his beautiful wife, tells them that Rebekah is his sister. But King Abimelech of Gerar (who earlier had the same trick pulled on him by Abraham and Sarah) looks out a window one day and sees Isaac playing around (Hebrew *kaheq*, KJV "sporting") with Rebekah. Called in, Isaac admits that Rebekah is his wife. Under Abimelech's protection thereafter, Isaac prospers in Gerar, till the locals grow so envious that Abimelech tells him to leave.

Settling in Beersheba, Isaac and Rebekah are crushed when their firstborn son Esau marries a Hittite woman. This prompts Rebekah to help Jacob, through deception, obtain the dying Isaac's blessing, and thus supplant the firstborn Esau. Jacob will father the twelve tribes of Israel, while Esau has to settle for founding Edom.

As for Isaac, he dies at the age of one hundred and eighty, the only Hebrew patriarch, as Jeremiah Unterman notes, who was monogamous and had no concubines.

(GEN. 24-26, 27:1-38)   ⇒ JACOB AND LABAN'S DAUGHTERS

ISAIAH: "Tremble, Ye Women"

When Israel and Syria invade Judah in 734 B.C.E., for Judah's refusal to join a defensive alliance against Assyria, the heart of Judah's king Ahaz is faint. Yahweh sends the prophet Isaiah and his son Shearjashub to King Ahaz to give him some signs.

The first sign (7:1-9) is Isaiah's offspring himself, whose name Shearjashub means "a remnant shall return." Ahaz should understand by this that his people will not be completely wiped out. Isaiah then tells Ahaz, "Ask thee a sign of the Lord thy God," but Ahaz is too weak-kneed to ask. Isaiah then angrily gives him a second sign (7:10-17). "Behold, a young woman shall conceive and bear a son," says Isaiah, "and you shall call his name Immanuel." (This is later interpreted by the Gospel of Matthew—out of context, and through mistranslation of "young woman" [Hebrew *alma*] as "virgin" [Greek *parthenos*]—as a prophecy of the virgin birth of Christ [see VIRGIN BIRTH: "CHILD OF THE HOLY GHOST"].) Before the child Immanuel ("God is with us") is old enough to know good from evil, Isaiah prophesies, the land will no longer be under siege.

The Lord now commissions a third sign (8:1-4), for which Isaiah commissions help from his wife ("the prophetess"). She conceives and bears a son. Yahweh tells Isaiah, "Call his name Maher-shalal-hash-baz," a mouthful meaning "the spoil and prey hasten." For before Maher-shalal-hash-baz is old enough to say Da-da and Ma-ma ("my father, and my mother"), the wealth of Damascus (capital of Syria) and Samaria (capital of Israel) will be carried away by Assyria.

Isaiah later becomes a sign himself, to Egypt and Ethiopia, by walking naked and barefoot for three years. So shall the king of Assyria lead away Egyptian and Ethiopian captives, "with their buttocks uncovered" (20:3-4).

Isaiah, like Hosea before him, refers to the Israelite people collectively as Yahweh's wife (54:5), a metaphor to be used also by Jeremiah and Ezekiel. He calls unfaithful Jerusalem "a harlot" (1:21), and warns that the people will pay dearly for cheating on Yahweh with their idolatry and foreign alliances. "Tremble, ye women," says Isaiah (32:11), for "ye shall conceive chaff, ye shall bring forth stubble" (33:11). The Lord will uncover "the secret parts" of the "daughters of Zion" (3:17), children will be slaughtered, and men will see "their wives ravished" (13:16; on the troubling nature of these images, see RAPE: "LEWDNESS AND FOLLY IN ISRAEL" and YAHWEH: "THY MAKER IS THINE HUSBAND"). Yet Isaiah also prophesies reconciliation and progeny: "I will bring forth a seed out of Jacob," says Yahweh (65:9), "I will loose the loins of kings" (45:1), and "all the seed of Israel," the "offspring of thy bowels," shall be "seed which the Lord hath blessed" (45:25; 48:19; 61:9).

(ISAIAH)   ⇒ SARAH AND TOBIAS

ISRAEL: "Beget Sons and Daughters"

In his old age the Hebrew patriarch Jacob, whom Yahweh has long since renamed Israel ("he who strives with God"), moves from Canaan to Egypt with eleven sons and their families (Gen. 46:8-27; Ex. 1:1-5). They are welcome in Egypt, for there Jacob's long-lost favorite son Joseph, sold into slavery by his jealous brothers, now governs as the Pharoah's prime minister (see JOSEPH AND POTIPHAR'S WIFE). But Jacob/Israel's descendants wear out this welcome with a population explosion. The Bible in effect describes the Hebrews in Egypt as breeding like rabbits: "And the children of Israel were fruitful, and increased abundantly, and multiplied, . . . and the land was filled with them" (Ex. 1:7). The Egyptians try enslavement as a birth control method, but this only adds fuel to the fire—"the more (the Egyptians) afflicted them, the more (the Hebrews) multiplied and grew" (Ex. 1:12).

This leads eventually to the Exodus: the Israelite people are led out of Egypt by Moses. Yahweh, as if now wondering himself how many Hebrews there are, orders Moses to do a census, counting all the Hebrew males age twenty and older. But the resulting number (hence "the book of Numbers") is over six hundred thousand (Num. 1:46; 2:32; 26:51), which is unrealistically high. (Five or six thousand adult Hebrew males would be more like it; see the notes on Numbers ch. 1 in Metzger and Murphy.) Whatever the actual number, all the men of the Exodus except Joshua and Caleb die during a forty-year wandering in the wilderness. Some of them die from plagues as punishment for orgiastic idolatry at Mount Sinai (see AARON AND THE GOLDEN CALF) and "whoredom" with the daughters of Moab (see COZBI AND ZIMRI). When the Israelites reach Canaan, their new leader Joshua conducts a mass circumcision—at a place appropriately called the "hill of the foreskins"—of the new generation of males born since the Exodus (Josh. 5:2-9; see CIRCUMCISION: "SIGN OF THE COVENANT").

The Hebrews invade Canaan, the land promised by Yahweh to their forefather Abraham (Gen. 12:7, 26:3), though the incursion is less a sweeping conquest (as idealized in the book of Joshua) than a tumultuous settling-in with the land's inhabitants (as reflected in Judges). The Israelites are commanded in Deuteronomy not to intermarry with the Canaanites, for "God hath chosen thee to be a special people unto himself," and intermarriage will lead to apostasy (7:2-8). And indeed, though Israel—becoming a monarchy (soon divided into the kingdoms of Israel and Judah)—gains ascendancy in the land, Canaanite religious practices remain such a temptation to the Hebrews that Israel, "as a backsliding heifer" (Hosea 4:16), habitually goes "a-whoring," a favorite biblical term for idolatry (see HARLOTRY).

For her idolatrous ways, compounded by questionable political alliances with foreigners, Israel is portrayed by the prophets—beginning with Hosea—not only as a harlot but as an unfaithful wife, whom husband Yahweh shall violently punish. (On this seeming endorsement of domestic violence, see YAHWEH: "THY MAKER IS THINE HUSBAND.")

Final punishment for the northern kingdom of Israel is destruction by Assyrian invaders, instruments of the cuckolded Yahweh, in 722 B.C.E. The southern kingdom, Israel's "treacherous sister Judah" (Jer. 3:8), is also guilty of playing the harlot (see JEREMIAH: "THY LOVERS WILL DESPISE THEE"), and falls to the Babylonians in 587 B.C.E.

In the wake of these catastrophes, however, the Old Testament prophets offer words of hope, prophesying Israel's restoration. "Take ye wives, and beget sons and daughters," declares Yahweh, for "I will sow the house of Israel and the house of Judah with the seed of man, and with the seed of beast" (Jer. 29:6, 31:27), and all the seed of Israel shall "be justified, and shall glory" (Isa. 45:25). "Let them put away their whoredom," Yahweh says of his people, "and I will dwell in their midst forever" (Ezek. 43:9).

J

JACOB AND LABAN'S DAUGHTERS

In his old age the Hebrew patriarch Isaac, at the urging of his wife Rebekah, sends their second son Jacob from Canaan to find a wife in Mesopotamia ("Paddanaram"). They do not want Jacob marrying a daughter of the Canaanites—their first son Esau has already married two Hittite women, to Isaac and Rebekah's "grief of mind." (More importantly, Rebekah wants to get Jacob away because his "hairy" brother Esau, the eventual founder of Edom, plans to kill him.)

Jacob has an auspicious dream on the very first night of his journey to Mesopotamia. He dreams of a stairway to heaven, with angels ascending and descending, and the Hebrew God Yahweh himself telling Jacob, "Thy seed shall be as the dust of the earth, . . . and in thy seed shall all the families of the earth be blessed." ("Kings," God tells Jacob years later in person, "shall come out of thy loins.")

Jacob reaches Haran, the Hebrews' ancestral Mesopotamian home, and stops to ask shepherds at a well about an uncle named Laban. Who should come along now but Rachel, a lovely maiden tending her father Laban's flock of sheep. When Jacob lays eyes on her (and on her father's wealth of sheep), he immediately falls in love. Jacob waters the sheep, kisses Rachel, cries, then finally introduces himself. Rachel runs to tell Laban, who comes running to welcome this kinsman from Canaan.

Jacob goes to work for Laban. "I will serve thee seven years," Jacob tells him, "for Rachel thy younger daughter."

Laban, who has an older daughter named Leah, agrees, and
Jacob puts in the seven years, though they seem like only "a few
days" because of his love for Rachel.

On the wedding night Jacob is given his veiled woman and,
as the Bible often describes sexual intercourse, "he went in unto
her." Jacob then awakes in the morning to behold her face,
and—it's Leah!

"What is this thou hast done unto me?" Jacob asks Laban,
who replies that in "our country" one must not "give the younger before the firstborn." Laban then lets him have Rachel too
on condition that Jacob serve him for seven more years. Thus
Jacob "went in also unto Rachel," says Genesis, and loved
"Rachel more than Leah."

The Lord, seeing that "Leah was hated," blesses her with
fertility, and she bears Jacob four sons, while Rachel remains
barren. "Give me children," the envious Rachel says to Jacob,
"or else I die." To which Jacob retorts, "Am I in God's stead,
who hath withheld from thee the fruit of the womb?"

Rachel resorts to the custom of using a concubine as a
surrogate child-bearer. "Behold my maid Bilhah, go in unto
her," Rachel tells Jacob, "and she shall bear upon my knees,
that I may also have children by her."

Jacob dutifully goes into Bilhah, who conceives and bears a
son. This makes Rachel so happy ("God," she exults, "hath
given me a son") that Jacob goes into Bilhah again. Bilhah bears
a second son, which Rachel also calls her own, while Leah is
apparently no longer fertile. "I wrestled with my sister," brags
Rachel, "and I have prevailed."

This is too much for Leah, who has Jacob go into her
handmaid Zilpah. This concubine bears two sons, whom Leah
names Gad ("fortune") and Asher ("happy"), saying "Happy
am I!"

The sibling rivalry continues. Rachel asks Leah to give her
some of the mandrakes—plant roots believed to promote fertility—that Leah's oldest son Reuben one day finds in the field
and brings home. "Is it a small matter," responds Leah, "that
thou hast taken my husband? and wouldest thou take away my

son's mandrakes also?"

Rachel proposes a deal: Jacob "shall lie with thee tonight," she tells Leah, if Leah will give Rachel the mandrakes.

Leah hands over the mandrakes. That evening she eagerly goes to meet Jacob—heading home from another day's work for Laban—with the news: "Thou must come in unto me." He has been "hired," Leah tells him, with the mandrakes.

It proves to be a good deal for both sisters. Leah proceeds to bear three more sons and a daughter, while Rachel also conceives and bears a son, God at last having "opened her womb." She names the son Joseph ("he adds"), for God, says Rachel, "shall add to me another son." But after Jacob has taken his wives and children home to Canaan, Rachel dies giving birth to her second son. She lives long enough to name him Benoni ("son of my sorrow"), a name that Jacob changes to Benjamin.

Jacob does not leave Laban's service, incidentally, without paying him back for deception. In the one biblical passage that describes animals having sex, Jacob produces stronger animals for himself, and weaker ones for Laban, by manipulating what the animals see while they're breeding. (On Rachel's theft of her father Laban's *teraphim*, see MENSTRUATION: SEVEN LONELY DAYS.)

In all Jacob—who also earns the name Israel, "he who strives with God," by literally wrestling with the Lord at Peniel (Gen. 32:24-30)—has twelve sons and one daughter by Laban's daughters and their handmaids. The sons are the ancestors of the twelve tribes of Israel. Interestingly, Reuben loses his pre-eminence among the tribes by committing incest (he has sex with his father's concubine Bilhah [Gen. 35:22; 49:3-4]), a transgression under the later Holiness Code (Lev. 17-26) of which Jacob himself is guilty. A man shall not "vex" his wife, says Lev. 18:18, by marrying her sister while the wife lives. Jacob certainly vexes Leah and Rachel! (See INCEST: "COME LIE WITH ME, MY SISTER.")   (GEN. 28-30; 35:16-26)   ⇒ SHECHEM AND DINAH

JEHORAM AND ATHALIAH

See ATHALIAH AND JEHORAM.

JEPHTHAH'S DAUGHTER

See VIRGINITY: "THE BRIDEGROOM REJOICETH."

JEREMIAH: "Thy Lovers Will Despise Thee"

The prophet Jeremiah portrays the kingdom of Judah in the sixth century B.C.E. as a promiscuous woman, a wife of Yahweh who commits adultery by worshipping other gods. "Thou hast played the harlot with many lovers," Jeremiah tells Judah, "and hast scattered thy ways to the strangers under every green tree" (3:1). Jeremiah also has choice words for the kingdom's males—they are "all adulterers, an assembly of treacherous men" (9:2), gathered "by troops in the harlots' houses," each man neighing like a horse for his neighbor's wife (5:7-8)—but the adulterous woman is the image that is predominantly used. "Where have you not been lain with?" Jeremiah asks Judah (3:2). "How can you say 'I am not defiled, I have not gone after Baalim'?" (2:23). Jeremiah even likens Judah to "a wild ass" in heat: "who can turn her away? . . . in her month they shall find her" (2:24).

Yahweh asks the "backsliding" people, who have "wrought lewdness with many" (11:15), to come back to him, "for I am married unto you" (3:14); but because Judah persists in her idolatry—committing "adultery with stones and with stocks" (3:9)—as did her backsliding sister Israel before her, Jeremiah prophesies disaster for Judah and her capital city. "Woe unto thee, O Jerusalem!" (13:27) for the pain that is coming will be like that of "a woman in travail" (13:21; 22:23; 31:8; 49:24). Yahweh, Jerusalem is told, will shame her, he will lift her skirts up over her face (13:26). "In vain shalt thou make thyself fair" with crimson dress, gold ornaments, and painted face, the Lord tells the city, for "thy lovers will despise thee, they will seek thy life" (4:30). Just as Samaria, the capital of adulterous Israel, fell to the Assyrians (722 B.C.E.), so the Babylonians "shall come and set fire" to Jerusalem for her idolatry and other wicked works (32:28-31).

Jerusalem is indeed destroyed (587 B.C.E.), with Judah's leading citizens either killed or taken into exile over the course of three Babylonian invasions. But to the survivors Jeremiah, having foretold such destruction, speaks of reconciliation and renewal. "Yea, I have loved thee with an everlasting love," says Yahweh, and "will save thee from afar, and thy seed" (31:3, 30:10); "ye shall be my people, and I will be your God," and again "shall the virgin rejoice in the dance" (30:22, 31:13).

(JEREMIAH)   ⇒ EZEKIEL

JERUSALEM: "As a Bride Adorned"

"How the faithful city has become a harlot!" So the prophet Isaiah (1:21) describes Jerusalem (also called Zion), capital of the kingdom of Judah, in the seventh century B.C.E. For the Judahites' idolatry, foreign intrigue, and social injustices, Yahweh, says Isaiah, "will smite with a scab the crown of the head of the daughters of Zion, and the Lord will discover their secret parts" (3:17). Jerusalem's women have been walking "with stretched forth necks and wanton eyes," but now "the Lord will take away the brave tinkling of their ornaments," stink will replace their "sweet smell," and there will be baldness instead of "well set hair" (3:16,18,24). "Thy men shall fall by the sword," Isaiah tells them, and in that desolate time "seven women shall take hold of one man" and beg to be called by his name (3:25-26).

Female wantonness as a metaphor for Jerusalem's unfaithfulness to Yahweh is also employed by the prophet Jeremiah in the late seventh and early sixth centuries, leading up to the city's destruction (587 B.C.E.). "Woe unto thee, O Jerusalem!" says the Lord, for "I have seen thine adulteries and thy neighings, the lewdness of thy whoredom, and thine abominations on the hills in the fields," and for this "will I discover thy skirts upon thy face, that thy shame may appear" (Jer. 13:26,27). Jerusalem, says Yahweh in Jeremiah, shall be given "into the hand of Nebuchadrezzar king of Babylon," whose army shall burn it, destroying the houses "upon whose roofs (the people) have offered incense unto Baal, and poured out drink offerings to other gods, to provoke me to anger" (32:28-29).

The prophet Ezekiel, writing before Jerusalem's fall as well as in Babylonian exile afterward, dwells at length on two sexually charged images of the city. In chapter 16, Jerusalem is a girl born in Canaan to Amorite and Hittite parents, who abandon her at birth; as a young maiden, naked and bloodied, she is found by Yahweh, who cleans her up, decks her with "excellent ornaments," and takes her as his wife. But she turns out to be a "whorish woman," committing fornication with Egyptian, Assyrian, and Babylonian lovers, whom she even pays for their services. In chapter 23, Jerusalem is a woman named Oholibah, who like her older sister Oholah (representing the fallen Israelite capital of Samaria) is a bride of Yahweh and bears him children, but then backslides precipitously into the "whoredoms" of her youth. (See EZEKIEL.)

Female imagery is used also in Lamentations, traditionally ascribed to Jeremiah, to describe Jerusalem's desolation after its fall into Babylonian hands. "I called for my lovers," says the ruined city, "but they deceived me" (1:19). The Babylonians "ravished the women in Zion" (4:4), and "the virgins of Jerusalem hang down their heads to the ground" (2:2). Those who honored Jerusalem "have seen her nakedness" and despise her (1:8); "her filthiness is in her skirts" (1:9), "Jerusalem is as a menstruous woman" (1:17). "From the daughter of Zion all her beauty is departed" (1:6), for the Lord himself "hath trodden the virgin . . . as in a winepress" (1:15), and there is "none to comfort her" (1:1). (On the problem of divine punishment portrayed as violence toward women, see YAHWEH.)

But there is also hope and assurance expressed in the prophets that Jerusalem the fallen woman shall be raised up again. "They called thee an Outcast," the city is told in Jeremiah, "saying, This is Zion, whom no man seeketh after" (30:17). But Jerusalem will be built again "upon her own heap"; she will "dwell safely," and her name will be "The Lord (is) our righteousness" (30:18, 33:16). Ezekiel also foresees a glorious new city, to be named "The Lord is there" (48:35). "Say ye to the daughter of Zion, Behold, thy salvation cometh," commands Isaiah (62:11), who has yet another new name for the city: "Thou shalt no more be termed Forsaken ... but thou shalt be called Hephzibah ('My delight is in her'), and thy land Beulah ('Married')." For "as the bridegroom rejoiceth over the bride, so shall thy God rejoice over thee" (62:4-5).

The imagery of bridegroom and bride returns in the book of Revelation: "And I John saw the holy city, new Jerusalem, coming down from God out of heaven, prepared as a bride adorned for her husband" (21:2). In John's vision, the husband is Christ "the Lamb" (19:7), and "the Lamb's wife" (21:9), symbolizing the Christian church, is the new Jerusalem.

JESUS CHRIST: There Ain't No Sex In Heaven

Did Jesus have a sex life? Ever since Chalcedon (a fifth-century ecumenical council), it has been the orthodox Christian view that Jesus was "truly God" and "truly man." (See also VIRGIN BIRTH: "CHILD OF THE HOLY GHOST.") The Chalcedon definition was a response to Monophysitism, the heretical view that Christ had a divine nature only. Fully human (and more), Jesus, says normative Christianity, shared human needs and desires; born "according to the flesh" (Rom. 1:4), he was "in all things like his brethren" (Heb. 2:17).

Yet despite his humanity and the many women whom his ministry attracted, the Bible is silent on any sexual involvement of Jesus. Moreover, statements attributed to Jesus regarding sex are basically negative. Thus a lustful thought is itself adultery (Matt. 5:28). Jesus is liberal in not condemning the woman taken in adultery, but he commands her to "sin no more" (John 8:3-11.) (He does not accuse the Samaritan woman, living with a man out of wedlock, of immorality, but that may be because she changes the subject when Jesus brings it up [John 4:5-26].) Jesus even refers to "eunuchs for the kingdom of heaven's sake" (Matt. 19:12), an apparent endorsement of sexual abstinence for those so inclined. Others should perhaps enjoy sex while they can, for Luke 20:33-36 quotes Jesus as saying there will be no marriage in the resurrection. In other words, there ain't no sex in heaven.

It can be argued that the ascetic portrayal of Christ in the gospels reflects not the historical Jesus but an antisexual attitude, under Hellenistic influences, that developed in the early church. One can then try reading between the lines for a sex life of Jesus, and it's intriguing what some people find. The Rev. John Williams, for example, finds what we might call the Gay Galilean. As Anglican Bishop Hugh Montefiore did some thirty years earlier, Williams suspects a homosexual lover in the unnamed "beloved disciple" in the Gospel of John (see HOMO-SEXUALITY: "THAT WHICH IS UNSEEMLY"). This would also explain why Jesus was unmarried, since Jewish rabbis and priests customarily had wives. But then Protestant theologian William E. Phipps and Episcopal Bishop John Shelby Spong suggest that Jesus *was* married. (On the missus most likely, see MARY, CALLED MAGDALENE). The Australian author Barbara Thiering not only has Jesus marrying Mary of Magdala, who bears him three children, but then has her divorcing him, after which Jesus weds Lydia, a traveling saleswoman who later entertains Paul (Acts 16:14-15). This might have made a good novel, but Thiering's work is classed as nonfiction.

Theories or fantasies about Jesus' sex life must remain speculation. And among conservative Christians one can still find some Monophysites in sheep's clothing. To them, the very idea of a sexually active Jesus, giving in to erotic desire, is taking

1 John 4:7, "Let us love one another," too far. (Consider the highly publicized furor over the 1988 film version of Nikos Kazantzakis's novel *The Last Temptation of Christ*, in which Jesus only *dreams* about having sex.)

The Bible goes pretty far, though, metaphorically. As Yahweh takes Israel as his bride (Isa. 54:5; 62:4-5; Ezek. 16), so Christ's love for the church is compared to that of a man for his wife (Eph. 5:22-32). "I have espoused you to one husband," Paul tells the Corinthian church, "that I may present you as a chaste virgin to Christ" (2 Cor. 11:2). In the Apocalypse, "the holy city, new Jerusalem," is "the Lamb's wife," descending from heaven "as a bride adorned for her husband" (Rev. 21:2, 9-10). "The marriage of the Lamb is come," says Saint John, "and his wife hath made herself ready" (Rev. 19:7). The love imagery becomes sexually explicit in the Song of Solomon, insofar as the lovers in that fine piece of Old Testament erotica have down through the ages been interpreted by many as an allegory of Christ and the church. (See SONG OF SOLOMON.)

⇒ MARY, CALLED MAGDALENE

JEZEBEL: "This Cursed Woman"

See AHAB AND JEZEBEL.

JOHN THE BAPTIST

See ELIZABETH AND ZECHARIAH *and* HEROD AND THE DANCE OF SALOME.

JOSEPH AND MARY

See VIRGIN BIRTH: "CHILD OF THE HOLY GHOST."

JOSEPH AND POTIPHAR'S WIFE

Jacob's six sons by his concubines Bilhah and Zilpah (he has four older sons by Leah) resent the fact that his favorite son is seventeen-year-old Joseph, "the son of his old age" by Rachel. They see the fine coat Joseph wears while helping them tend the flocks; they hear of the "evil report" he makes about them to his father; and they have to listen to him recount his dreams, such as that of the sun, moon, and stars bowing down to him. They finally have enough of "this dreamer" and sell him for twenty shekels of silver to some Ishmaelites passing through Canaan. Joseph's fancy coat they dip in blood and take to Jacob, who mournfully assumes that the lad has been devoured by some wild beast.

Joseph is taken to Egypt, where the Ishmaelites sell him to Potiphar, an officer of the Pharoah. Seeing that "the Lord made all that (Joseph) did to prosper in his hand," Potiphar makes Joseph the overseer of his house. And day after day, while the master's away, Potiphar's wife tries to lure the Hebrew into bed. "Lie with me," she tells him, but Joseph resists the temptation, if there is any. "How can I do this great wickedness," he asks her, "and sin against God?"

Finally one day she grabs Joseph by his garment. "Lie with me," she repeats, but Joseph flees, leaving the garment in her hand. Hell having no fury like a woman scorned (according to the dramatist William Congreve), Potiphar's wife cries out for the men of her household. They come and she shows them the garment. "He has brought in a Hebrew to mock us," she says of her husband. She claims that Joseph came "to lie with" her, and that he ran away, leaving his garment, when she screamed.

When Potiphar comes home and hears his wife's lie, he angrily has Joseph thrown into prison. In almost no time at all, though, Joseph is running the prison. He also has a knack for interpreting dreams, which wins him the Pharoah's favor. The Pharoah soon puts Joseph in charge of the whole land of Egypt. He also gives him Asenath, the daughter of Potiphera, priest of

1. THE EARTHLY PARADISE

S. Marmion, from *Le Livre des sept âges du monde*
(manuscript 9047, fol. 1r), before 1467
Copyright Bibliothèque royale Albert 1er, Bruxelles

In the first creation account in Genesis (1:1-2:3), God creates man and woman simultaneously ("male and female created he them"), and commands them to "be fruitful and multiply."

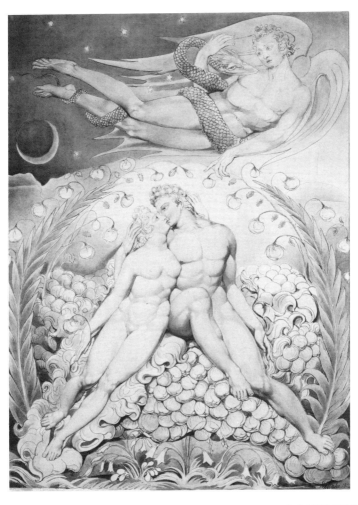

2. SATAN WATCHING THE CARESSES OF ADAM AND EVE

William Blake (1757-1827)
Gift by Subscription, 1890. Courtesy, Museum of Fine Arts, Boston

Given God's commandment to reproduce, it was natural for Adam and Eve to make love in the Garden of Eden, though the verse "And Adam knew Eve his wife, and she conceived, and bare Cain" (Gen. 4:1) occurs after the Fall.

3. THE FALL OF MAN

Palma il Giovane (1544-1628)
Walters Art Gallery, Baltimore

Disobedience, not sex, leads to Adam and Eve's Fall, though after loss
of innocence they are to become self-conscious about being naked
(Gen. 3:7).

4. LOT AND HIS DAUGHTERS

Bonifazio de' Pitati (1487-1553)
The Chrysler Museum, Norfolk, VA
Gift of Walter P. Chrysler, Jr., 71.622

Following God's destruction of Sodom, Lot's two daughters get their
father drunk in order to lie with him and thereby have children. (Gen.
19:30-38)

5. REBECCA AT THE WELL

Giovanni Antonio Pellegrini (1675-1741)
Reproduced by courtesy of the Trustees,
The National Gallery, London

Abraham's servant, sent to the Mesopotamian town of Nahor to find
a wife for Isaac, runs right into Rebekah, "very fair to look upon, a
virgin, neither had any man known her" (Gen. 24:16).

6. JOSEPH AND POTIPHAR'S WIFE

Paolo Finoglia (c. 1590-1645)
Courtesy of the Fogg Art Museum, Harvard University Art Museums
Gift of Samuel H. Kress Foundation

"And she caught him by his garment, saying, Lie with me: and he left his garment in her hand, and fled, and got him out" (Gen. 39:12). For spite she then falsely accuses him of trying to lie with her.

7. JUDAH AND TAMAR

Horace Vernet (1789-1863)
Reproduced by permission of the Trustees
of the Wallace Collection, London

Judah unwittingly acquires firsthand knowledge that his daughter-in-
law Tamar has "played the harlot" (Gen. 38:15,18).

8. THE WORSHIP OF THE GOLDEN CALF

Jan Steen (1626-1679). North Carolina Museum of Art, Raleigh,
Purchased with funds from the state of North Carolina

The children of Israel often go "a-whoring after other gods" (Judg.
2:17). Below Mount Sinai they worship a golden calf—made for them
by Aaron while Moses is away on the mountain—with a feast and
sexual "play" (Exodus 32).

9. SAMSON AND DELILAH

Claude Mellan (1598-1688)
The Metropolitan Museum of Art,
Harris Brisbane Dick Fund, 1917 (17.3.1125)

His lover Delilah betrays Samson while he sleeps on her knees (Judg. 16:19).

10. THE LETTER

Jan Steen (1626-1679)
Virginia Museum of Fine Arts, Richmond, VA
The Adolph D. and Wilkins C. Williams Fund

King David sends for Bathsheba, after watching her bathe one night
from his roof. Impregnating her, David marries Bathsheba after
arranging the death of her husband. (2 Sam. 11:2-12:24)

11. AMNON AND TAMAR

Giovanni Francesco Barbieri, called Guercino (1591-1666)
Patrons' Permanent Fund, © 1994 Board of Trustees,
National Gallery of Art, Washington, D.C.

King David's son Amnon, pretending to be sick, rapes Tamar, his
half-sister who attends him. Tamar's full brother Absalom will later
take vengeance. (2 Sam. 13:1-29)

12. THE WEDDING NIGHT OF TOBIAS AND SARAH

Pieter Lastman (1583-1633)
Juliana Cheney Edwards Collection
Courtesy, Museum of Fine Arts, Boston

Before sleeping with Sarah, Tobias smokes out a demon who has killed Sarah's previous seven husbands on their wedding nights. (Tobit, the Apocrypha)

13. SUSANNAH AND THE ELDERS

Giuseppe Bartolomeo Chiari (1654-1727)
Walters Art Gallery, Baltimore

Bathing in the garden, Susanna is surprised by two elders who come
out of hiding. "We are in love with you," they tell her, "so lie with us"
(Susanna 20, the Apocrypha).

14. THE CIRCUMCISION

Parmigianino (1503-1540)
© The Detroit Institute of Arts
Gift of Axel Beskow

In keeping with Hebrew law (Gen. 17:12), Jesus is circumcised and named when he is eight days old (Luke 2:21).

15. CHRIST AND THE WOMAN TAKEN IN ADULTERY

Max Beckmann (1884-1950)
The Saint Louis Art Museum

The scribes and Pharisees bring an adulteress to Jesus. Reminding
him that the woman should be stoned to death according to Mosaic
law, they ask Christ his opinion. "Let him who is without sin among
you," he replies, "cast the first stone." (John 8:3-11)

16. THE MAGDALENE

Bernardino Luini (c. 1480-1532)
Samuel H. Kress Collection, © 1995 Board of Trustees,
National Gallery of Art, Washington, D.C.

A group of biblical scholars called the Jesus Seminar believes that
Jesus and "Mary called Magdalene, out of whom went seven devils"
(Luke 8:2), likely had "a special relationship"—though the evidence
is biblically lacking.

the sun god Re, in marriage. (In the pseudepigraphical Joseph
and Aseneth, Joseph refuses to marry this Egyptian priest's
daughter until she converts from her idolatry; see Burchard.)

Asenath bears Joseph two sons, Manasseh and Ephraim.
They are later adopted by their grandfather Jacob, who is
reunited with Joseph in Egypt. Joseph's sons thus join Jacob's
twelve natural sons (Benjamin having been added by Rachel)
as ancestors of the twelve tribes of Israel (the tribe of Joseph
becoming the two tribes of Manasseh and Ephraim).

(GEN. 37, 39-41, 47-48)   ⇒ MOSES AND ZIPPORAH

JUDAH AND TAMAR

Jacob's fourth son Judah, praised by his father as "a lion's
whelp" (Gen. 49:9), goes to visit a friend named Hirah in the
Canaanite town of Adullam. While there Judah is attracted to
the daughter of a man named Shuah. Taking her as his wife,
Judah, we are told, "went in unto her." She bears a son named
Er, for whom Judah in due course finds a wife. Judah's Canaanite wife conceives twice more, bearing sons Onan and Shelah.

Judah's eldest son Er turns out to be a lion's whelp himself:
"the Lord slew him," the Bible says, for being "wicked." As Er
leaves no children, Judah tells second son Onan to marry Er's
widow Tamar. This is in keeping with the Hebrew levirate law
(from *levir*, "brother-in-law"), according to which the brother
of a man who dies childless shall marry the widow to give his
dead brother offspring (Deut. 25:5-10). But Onan resents the
fact that the offpsring so produced will not be considered his.
So when Onan has sexual intercourse with Tamar, he deliberately
spills his semen on the ground. He is then slain by the Lord for not
properly discharging his duty. (See ONAN AND TAMAR.)

Judah tells Er's and Onan's widow Tamar to go live with her
father till third son Shelah is old enough to be next. But when
the boy is grown, Judah, understandably reluctant to have a third
son marry this woman, does not give Tamar to Shelah.

There is another death (apparently unrelated) in the family, Judah losing his Canaanite wife. But there is still lots of life left in Judah. On a trip to Timnath for a sheepshearing, Judah spots a veiled woman sitting on the wayside. Assuming she's a prostitute, he stops to proposition her: "Go to, I pray thee, let me come in unto thee.'"

"What wilt thou give me," she asks, "that thou mayest come in unto me?"

"I will send thee a kid from the flock," says Judah.

She asks if he will give her something as a pledge till the kid is delivered. "What pledge shall I give thee?" he asks.

She requests his signet, bracelets, and staff, which Judah promptly hands over. The two then have sexual intercourse.

When Judah later sends his friend Hirah the Adullamite to deliver the kid and recover his signet, bracelets, and staff, the woman is nowhere to be found. Hirah asks some men in the area about "the *qedeshah*" who had been on the wayside. Their reply: "There was no *qedeshah* in this place." (Hirah's use of the term *qedeshah*—literally "holy woman"—instead of *zonah*, the Hebrew word for a harlot, has historically been seen as evidence for the practice of sacred prostitution in ancient Israel. But it is unclear why Hirah uses the term. Since a holy woman or a harlot could either one have conceivably been there, perhaps Hirah asks folks about a "holy woman" because he prefers not to be asking about a "whore." See PROSTITUTION.)

Hirah has to inform Judah that he has apparently seen the last of his signet, bracelets, and staff. Soon Judah gets even more bad news: his daughter-in-law Tamar, someone tells him, has "played the harlot" and is pregnant. "Bring her forth," says Judah, "and let her be burnt."

When Tamar is brought forth, she brings forth with her Judah's signet, bracelets, and staff, and rhetorically asks "Whose are these?" Tamar, Judah now realizes, was the whore on the wayside—she had indeed "played" the harlot—and it is presumably his offspring she carries. Judah acknowledges his belongings, and the fact that Tamar—though she has tricked him, for the sake of offspring, into committing incest (Lev. 18:15)—is "more righteous" than he, for his failure to give her to Shelah.

Tamar bears twins named Perez and Zerah. While still in the womb, Zerah puts out his hand, as if to say "I'm first." The midwife accordingly ties a scarlet thread around Zerah's wrist. But then the hand goes back in, and Perez (whose descendants will include King David and Jesus) is born first.

Tamar is admired today as a woman who asserted her rights in a patriarchal society—albeit through deception—despite Judah's attempt to deny them. Yet, as Sharon Pace Jeansonne notes, there is a "lingering injustice" at the end of the story: it leaves Tamar as a single mother, still denied the husband she was promised, and with no hint of assistance from Judah. The statement that Judah "knew her again no more" implies social as well as sexual non-contact. In the pseudepigraphical Testament of Judah, the dying man states that after his experience with Tamar—whom he did not recognize on the road to Timnath, he says, because he was drunk at the time—he went to join his brother Joseph in Egypt, and did not go near Tamar for the rest of his life (12:1-2; see Kee).   (GENESIS 38)

⇒ JOSEPH AND POTIPHAR'S WIFE

JUDAH, THE KINGDOM OF

See ISRAEL: "BEGET SONS AND DAUGHTERS"; SOLOMON AND HIS "OUTLANDISH WOMEN"; MAACAH AND REHOBOAM; ATHALIAH AND JEHORAM; EZEKIEL: TALKING LEWD WOMEN; JEREMIAH: "THY LOVERS WILL DESPISE THEE"; *and* JERUSALEM: "AS A BRIDE ADORNED."

JUDITH AND HOLOFERNES

Talk about sex appeal, Judith has it. She is a beautiful woman, with a face so lovely that men marvel to behold it. And she's rich, her late husband Manasseh, dead from sunstroke, having left her with money, slaves, cattle, and fields. Yes, a man could easily lose his head over a woman like Judith (whose name in Hebrew means "Jewess" or "female Judean"). But though many desire her, she chooses to remain a widow, fasting regularly while maintaining her estate in the Judean town of Bethulia.

Judith also speaks wisely, and has plenty to say upon hearing that Bethulia's magistrates have decided to surrender the town to Assyrian invaders—who have besieged it for over a month and cut off the water supply—unless God intervenes in five days. (This invasion is an anachronism in the story, which is set in postexilic Judea, long after the demise of Assyria.) Judith summons the magistrates and upbraids them for testing God, who can protect his people whenever he wishes, by giving him a five-day deadline.

When the magistrate Uzziah points out that the people are dying of thirst, Judith replies that she is about to do something—something momentous that will be remembered, she says, for all generations—to take care of the situation.

That night Judith takes off her widow's garments, bathes, and anoints herself with fine ointment. She puts on a tiara, anklets, bracelets, and earrings, and the brightest of the clothes that she wore when her husband was living. She fills a bag with a bottle of wine, a flask of oil, and some food, and then, with her maid who carries the bag, Judith heads for the city gate.

At the gate Uzziah and the other elders are bedazzled by Judith's appearance. Praying that God will favor her plan, the elders open the gate for her, and watch as Judith and the maid proceed down through the valley till no longer in sight.

Judith is stopped by an Assyrian patrol, which marvels at her beauty as much as her story: she has fled Bethulia, and wants to tell Holofernes, commander of the Assyrian army, how he can take all of Judea without losing a single man.

Her gorgeous appearance excites the whole camp as she is escorted to Holofernes's tent. Who can hate the Hebrews, the Assyrians wonder, when they have women like this? The general Holofernes, relaxing on his canopied bed, is as struck by her

beauty as everyone else. When he graciously asks why she has
come, Judith tells him that her people in their hunger are
planning to break God's law by eating first fruits consecrated
for priestly use only. On the day that they do this, they will be
destroyed by the Assyrians. So she fled, and has been sent by
God to Holofernes. Staying with the Assyrians, she will go out
and pray each night in the valley, and God will tell her when the
Hebrews have sinned. She will tell Holofernes, who can then
march with his army all the way to Jerusalem, without so much
as a dog barking at him.

Holofernes likes what he hears. "Your God shall be my
God," he tells her, and on each of the next three nights Judith
is allowed to leave the camp unhindered to go pray in the valley.
Holofernes also likes what he sees, of course, and on the fourth
night is determined to have Judith in his canopied bed. It would
be a disgrace, he tells his eunuch Bagoas, to let such a woman go
without having her, and on top of that she would laugh at him.

That night Holofernes invites Judith, through Bagoas, to a
banquet in his tent. "Who am I," Judith replies through Bagoas,
"to refuse my lord?" While Judith gets dressed, her maid goes
and spreads fleeces on the ground before Holofernes, so that
Judith may recline while she eats.

When Judith, dressed to kill, comes in and lies down,
Holofernes can hardly control himself. He tells her to drink and
be merry, and Judith says, "I will indeed drink, my lord, for my
life this day means more to me than in all the days since I was
born." The excited Holofernes proceeds to drink more wine
than he has ever downed in his life, while Judith consumes
kosher food and drink from her food bag. By the time the other
guests leave, and Bagoas shuts the tent from outside, leaving
Judith alone with Holofernes, the general is stretched out on
his bed in a drunken stupor.

Judith takes down a sword from the wall. Stepping to the
bed, she takes the general by the hair of the head. Judith utters
a prayer, asking the Lord God for strength, and with two strokes
she cuts off Holofernes's head.

Judith puts the head in her food bag, which she hands to her maid waiting outside. Judith also takes the bed's canopy as a trophy. The two women proceed out of the camp, the Assyrians assuming that she is off again to her prayers. (How she transports the canopy is unstated.) Judith returns to Bethulia, where at dawn the head is hung up for display. The inspired Israelites go out to do battle, prompting Bagoas to go wake his master—and make a grisly discovery. The Assyrians are routed, and her people hail Judith as "the glory of Israel." ("It was my face that deceived him," she assures them, "he committed no sin with me, to defile and disgrace me.")

Judith, needless to say, is one of the most imposing figures, male or female, in Hebrew tradition. The story told in the book of Judith (found in the Apocrypha in the Catholic Bible) is similar to that of Jael, in the days when the prophetess Deborah judged Israel. As it is told in Judges (ch. 4), the Kenite woman Jael gives Sisera, a defeated Canaanite general fleeing from the Israelites, a place to hide in her tent, some milk to quench his thirst, and, after Sisera falls asleep, a tent peg through the head with a hammer. But unlike Judith, Jael does not use sex appeal to do in the villain. Jael kills him with kindness. (For discussion of sexual nuances in the Jael story, see Susan Niditch.)

(APOCRYPHA: JUDITH)   ⇒ ELIZABETH AND ZECHARIAH

K

KETURAH AND ABRAHAM

See ABRAHAM AND SARAH.

KISSING: "Better than Wine"

Most kisses referred to in the Bible are nonromantic gestures. These are usually kisses of greeting (as in Paul's "Greet one another with a holy kiss" [1 Cor. 16:20; 2 Cor. 13:12]), though they can turn out to be kisses of death: Judas betrays Christ with a kiss (Matt. 26:48-49; Mark 14:45-46; Luke 22:47-48), and Joab kisses Amasa just before disemboweling him (1 Sam. 20:9-10).

In Proverbs an adulteress catches and kisses "a young man void of understanding," luring him to her bed though "her house is the way to hell" (7:6-27). Though "the lips of a strange woman drop as an honeycomb, and her mouth is smoother than oil," says Proverbs, "her end is bitter as wormwood, sharp as a two-edged sword" (5:3-4).

The only positive biblical references to erotic kissing occur in the Song of Solomon: "Let him kiss me with the kisses of his mouth: for (his) love is better than wine" (1:2); "Thy lips, O my spouse, drop as the honeycomb: honey and milk are under thy tongue" (4:11); "His lips (are) like lilies, dropping sweet smelling myrrh" (5:13); "And the roof of thy mouth (is) like the best wine for my beloved, that goeth down sweetly" (7:9); "When I should find thee without, I would kiss thee" (8:1).

It may seem odd, with so much sex in the Bible, to find so little smooching. But while sex between man and wife is to be enjoyed (Prov. 5:18-19), it is portrayed as an act of procreation, following the commandment of Yahweh to "be fruitful and multiply" (Gen. 1:28); and the Bible, after all, is basically a religious history, not a historical romance. Thus the biblical writers spend no time describing foreplay—when it comes to fooling around, the Bible gets right to the point.

KNOWLEDGE (CARNAL)

See LOVEMAKING: TO KNOW IN THE BIBLICAL SENSE.

L

LAMECH, THE WORLD'S FIRST POLYGAMIST

There are two differing Lamech traditions in Genesis. In the first one, Lamech, a sixth-generation descendant of Adam and Eve, marries two women. This first recorded polygamist has three sons who accomplish firsts of their own: his first wife Adah bears Jabal, the world's first cattleman, and Jubal, the first player of musical instruments, while his other wife Zillah bears Tubalcain, the first instructor of metallurgy. Zillah also bears a daughter named Naamah, who, being a woman, is not credited with being the first of anything. (See GENDER.)

In the second tradition, Lamech is the son of Methuselah, the oldest man in the Bible. Like his father before him, this Lamech doesn't rush into parenthood: he is one hundred and eighty years old when he gets around to fathering Noah. Lamech finds time for more progeny during his remaining five hundred and ninety-five years. (After the birth of the Nephilim and Noah's Flood, people start living shorter lives [only gradually, though—see SHEM], no doubt part of God's judgment of man.)

(GEN. 4:19-24; 5:25-31)   ⇒ SONS OF GOD

LEAH: "Thou Hast Taken My Husband"

See JACOB AND LABAN'S DAUGHTERS.

LESBIANISM: "Against Nature"

In his epistle to the Romans (1:26-27), the Apostle Paul condemns what he calls "vile affections," referring to homosexuality both among males ("men with men working that which is unseemly") and females (women who "change the natural use [of their bodies] into that which is against nature").

While male homosexuality is condemned also in the Old Testament (Lev. 18:22, 20:13), Paul's is the only reference in the Bible to lesbianism. (It is roundabout because there is no single word in biblical Hebrew or Greek for homosexuality of either gender). It is possible that same-sex lovemaking among women is not mentioned in the Old Testament because sex between women, unlike sex between males, does not involve a wasting of seed, indeed does not involve males, and was therefore of no particular concern in ancient Israel's male-centered society. (For a lesbian interpretation of Ruth's devotion to Naomi in the book of Ruth, see Rebecca Alpert.)

LEVITE'S CONCUBINE, RAPE OF THE

See BENJAMIN: "A RAVENOUS WOLF."

LOT AND HIS DAUGHTERS

Following Yahweh's destruction of Sodom and other cities of the Jordan plain (see SODOM[Y[AND GOMORRAH), Abraham's nephew Lot and Lot's two daughters—formerly residents of Sodom—find themselves living in a cave. The older daughter expresses to the younger her fear that, for lack of a mate, they are now to be childless. "Our father is old, and there is not a man in the earth to come in unto us after the manner of all the earth."

Her words suggest that this story originally involved a world cataclysm, with Lot and his daughters, like Noah and his family in the flood story, being the only surviving humans. But the suggestion is academic, as her words make sense either way. These daughters have had a bad time. First they lose their married sisters in Sodom's supernatural fall, then their mother is lost—turned into a pillar of salt—in the flight from the scene of destruction. They then flee with their father from the city of Zoar—where according to Yahweh they were supposed to be safe—apparently because the destruction has spread, engulfing virtually the whole Jordan plain. Now languishing in their mountain cave, Lot's daughters might easily be excused for assuming that, save the old man, the rest of humanity has been wiped out by the wrath of God.

In any case Lot's daughters take action. "Come, let us make our father drink wine, and we will lie with him," says the older one, "that we may preserve seed of our father." So they get Lot drunk on successive nights, with the firstborn lying with him on the first night, and the younger one on the second night, with Lot remembering nothing about either occasion. Impregnated, the two daughters bear Moab, the father of the Moabites, and Benammi, the father of the Ammonites.

Thus Genesis, in the story of Lot and his daughters, pulls a rather sly little trick. It matter-of-factly presents two troublesome neighbors of Israel—Moab and Ammon, lying east of the Jordan River—as children of incest, without passing any judgment on the three incestuous Hebrew parents. (See INCEST.)

(GEN. 19:30-38)   ⇒ ISAAC AND REBEKAH

LOVEMAKING: To Know in the Biblical Sense

Survival for the biblical Hebrews depended not only on serving their God but on adequate numbers. For both reasons they took Yahweh's first commandment—"Be fruitful and multiply" (Gen. 1:28)—seriously. The Hebrews were high on reproduction; as Gene McAfee puts it, they had "a vigorous pronatalist worldview." But they also had God-given laws to help keep things in perspective. Thus the commandment against adultery protected property rights (women being subordinate and essentially owned by their husbands), and laws against incest protected the integrity of the family. Procreative pursuits were also affected by the ritual purity system. Genital emissions were considered in some sense "unclean," requiring purification of those emitting them and those who were affected thereby. Thus a man and a woman were to bathe in water after sexual intercourse if there had been an emission of semen, and they were considered ritually unclean for the day (Lev. 15:16-18). (The same applied to a man who chanced to have a nocturnal emission [Deut. 23:10-11].) Purity also required sexual abstinence during times of worship—"come not at your wives" (Ex. 19:15)—and warfare (1 Sam. 21:4-5; 2 Sam. 11:11). (A newly married man, however, was given a year off from war and other work, to stay home and "cheer up his wife" [Deut. 24:5].)

The Hebrew word for love in general is *ahabah* (verb form *aheb*). (God's love for his people is often called *hesed* [KJV "loving-kindness," RSV "steadfast love"].) For sexual intercourse, the Old Testament writers use the verb *bo* ("to enter" or "to go into") or the euphemisms "to lie with" (*yashav*) and "to know" (*yada*). ("To know" in this sense is subsequently found also in Greek, as *ginosko*.) These sexual terms occur many times in the Hebrew Bible, and typically each use covers the whole sexual encounter, any foreplay or other elaboration not being a narrative concern. (See KISSING.). Usually the only point seems to be that the lovers are about the task of being fruitful and multiplying (e.g., "And Adam knew Eve," who bears Cain [Gen. 4:1]), though at times the encounter, as far as the man is concerned, is for sexual gratification (see, for example, BATHSHEBA and JUDAH AND TAMAR).

Notable exceptions to such brief, matter-of-fact descriptions are diatribes against Israelite idolatry, conceived of as "playing the harlot" (Hebrew verb *zanah*) and using often lurid sexual imagery (see EZEKIEL). There is also the erotic Song of Solomon, in which the term for lovemaking or "caressing" is *dodim* (related to the word for female breasts), with the woman of the Song referring to the man as her *dodi* ("lover"). (*Dodim* is also used in Prov. 7:18, where an adulteress entices a young man with "Come, let us take our fill of love.")

The Greek New Testament reflects a different milieu. Gone is the "pronatalist worldview," replaced by the belief among the first Christians that the world is soon coming to an end (Matt. 16:28; 24:34; 1 Cor. 7:29-31; James 5:8). Gone also, under Hellenistic influence, is the Hebrew notion that a man should "rejoice with the wife of his youth" and be "ravished always" with her love (Prov. 5:18-19). Instead there is the misogynistic view that a woman should be seen and not heard, and that she is to be seen as uninvitingly as possible. Just as the Greek philosopher Aristotle, quoting some unnamed poet, wrote that "silence is a woman's glory" (see Ghougassian), so Christian women are to "keep silence in the churches" (1 Cor. 14:34); and just as Perictione cautioned Greek women against wearing fine clothes and bathing too often, so Christian women are to wear "modest apparel, with shamefacedness and sobriety" (1 Tim. 2:9). A husband is to love his wife (Col. 3:19, Eph. 5:26), and should have sex with her regularly to avoid infidelity (1 Cor. 7:2-5). But though it's "better to marry than to burn" with desire (1 Cor. 7:9), the best way sexually to await the world's end, says the Apostle Paul, is to be unmarried and celibate (1 Cor. 7:7-8). (The usual Greek word for romantic or sexual love, *eros*, is found nowhere in the New Testament; the word used for love is *agape*, which has a spiritual sense, with *philia* being brotherly love.) "It is good," Paul says in short (quoting the Corinthians), "for a man not to touch a woman" (1 Cor. 7:1)—which would no doubt sound strange to the just-married Old Testament warrior who got to spend a whole year with his wife. (See also PAUL.)

LUST: "Natural Brute Beasts"

See FLESH: "TO BE CARNALLY MINDED IS DEATH."

M

MAACHAH AND REHOBOAM

King Rehoboam of Judah loves Maachah "above all his wives and concubines." Considering the fact that Rehoboam has eighteen wives and sixty concubines (by whom he has twenty-eight sons and sixty daughters), Maachah has to be quite a woman.

But Maachah may also be a bad influence. For under Rehoboam, Judah does "evil in the sight of the Lord." Idolatry runs rampant, as the people erect high places, pillars, and sacred poles (*asherim*) "on every high hill, and under every green tree." The land is also full of *qedeshim*, cult functionaries forbidden by Yahweh—though "sodomites" (KJV) and "male temple prostitutes" (NRSV) are dubious translations of *qedeshim* (literally "holy ones"; see PROSTITUTION). In sum, the Judahites commit "all the abominations" of the Canaanites before them. (See Leviticus 18 for a list of these offenses.)

The extent of Maachah's influence is conjectural, but she is the mother of Abijah (aka Abijam), who, as king after Rehoboam's death, walks "in all the sins of his father" (and has almost as many wives). As queen mother Maachah outlives even Abijah. However, she runs afoul of her grandson Asa, who as king embarks on religious reform. Asa tears down an idol that Maachah has built in honor of Asherah—a goddess who may have been worshipped as a consort of Yahweh (see ASHE-RAH)—and ceremoniously burns it. Asa then deposes Maachah as queen mother.

Her reign thus ends in disgrace, and some reign it was. Yahweh's people had never gone "a-whoring after other gods" (see HARLOTRY) moreso than under Rehoboam (and Abijah) and his beloved queen Maachah.

(1 KGS. 14:21-24; 15:1-3,9-13; 2 CHR. 11:21-22)   ⇒ AHAB AND JEZEBEL

MAGDALENE, MARY

See MARY, CALLED MAGDALENE.

MANDRAKES: "Laid Up for Thee"

The flowering plant mandragora or mandrake, with a root fancied to resemble the human body, was believed in biblical times to be an aphrodisiac and fertility aid.

In Genesis, when her son Reuben brings Leah some mandrakes that he found in the field, her barren sister Rachel talks Leah out of them by letting her sleep that night with Jacob, the husband whom they share. Thus the mandrakes work for Leah after all, as she proceeds to have three more children before Rachel finally conceives one of her own (30:14-22).

In the Song of Solomon, the woman tells her lover that over the doors mandrakes and other "pleasant fruits" are "laid up for thee" (7:13). The Hebrew word for mandrakes is *duda'im*, which is appropriately similar to *dodim*, the word used in the Song for lovemaking. (See LOVEMAKING: TO KNOW IN THE BIBLICAL SENSE.)

MARRIAGE: "They Shall Be One Flesh"

"Therefore shall a man leave his father and his mother, and shall cleave to his wife: and they shall be one flesh." That's how

Genesis (2:24, quoted in Mark 10:7-8 and Eph. 5:31) idealizes marriage, an institution for which there is no single word in biblical Hebrew. In fact there are no words for "husband" and "wife," the Hebrew words so translated being *baal* ("master" or "lord") and *ishah* ("woman"), words that more clearly reflect the nature of biblical marriage. As discussed elsewhere (see GENDER), Hebrew society was patriarchal; its women were second-class citizens, treated basically as men's childbearing property. This status was scripturally a result of the Fall, with God telling Eve, "(Thy husband) shall rule over thee" (Gen. 3:16). A Hebrew man, moreover, could rule over more than one woman (see CONCUBINES: "MANY STRANGE WOMEN"). So a man and a woman in marriage may have been "one flesh," but it was more his flesh than hers, and was subject to more flesh being added. The only scriptural limit was that Hebrew men were not to marry non-Hebrew women, Yahweh having chosen Israel as "a special people unto himself" (Deut. 7:2-8). As in the case of Moses, this limit was often ignored. (See especially EZRA: "YE HAVE TAKEN STRANGE WIVES").

A young man or woman's first marriage was customarily arranged by the parents involved. The bridegroom's family provided the bride's father with a *mohar* or marriage price, at which time the bride, in Schiffman and Achtemeier's words, was "transferred" from her father's house "into her husband's juris-diction." The statement in Genesis that a man "shall leave his father and his mother and shall cleave to his wife" is misleading, as in fact a woman would leave her father and her mother and would cleave to her husband. As Raphael Patai notes, the husband would ordinarily not leave his father and his mother, but would stay on, eventually adding children of his own, as part of the large extended family typical of the biblical Hebrews.

While marriages were arranged, a young man, given the androcentric (male-centered) nature of biblical society, was in a better position than a woman to have his preference consid-ered. Thus Samson talks his parents into getting for him a Philistine woman (Judg. 14:2), and the Hivite Shechem asks his father to get for him the Hebrew Dinah, whom Shechem has already raped (see SHECHEM AND DINAH). The passive Isaac, on the other hand, has to settle for whomever a servant of his father brings back for him from Mesopotamia. Isaac lucks out, as the servant shows up with Rebekah.

A man could also win a particular woman as a prize. Thus Caleb offers his daughter Achsah as a wife to whomever takes the town of Debir during the conquest of Canaan. Achsah is won by Othniel, Caleb's nephew (Josh. 15:15-17; Judg. 1:11-13). Saul offers his daughter Michal to David if David can deliver one hundred Philistine foreskins. David brings in an extra hundred (1 Sam. 18:20-27).

Little is known of marriage ceremonies in biblical times other than what tidbits the Bible provides. We are told, for example, that the wedding feasts of Jacob and Samson each last seven days (Gen. 29:27-28; Judg. 14:10-12), and that of Tobias fourteen (Tobit 8:19-20). Jesus attends a wedding in Cana at which the guests guzzle down all the wine, necessitating divine intervention (John 2:1-10). Such festive consumption, combined with the bride's veil and the darkness, may explain how Jacob could spend his wedding night with the wrong woman and not know it till the following day (Gen. 29:21-25).

If a man took a wife and claimed that he "found her (to be) not a maid" (which meant she had "played the whore in her father's house"), and her father could not refute this by producing "the tokens of (her) virginity" (a bloodied bed cloth from her wedding night), the law called for the woman to be stoned to death. But if the man was judged to have lied, thus bringing "an evil name upon a virgin of Israel," he would be whipped, had to pay her father a hundred shekels of silver, and had to keep the woman for the rest of his life (Deut. 22:13-21).

A man didn't have to lie to get out of a marriage, as simply not liking something about one's wife was sufficient grounds, according to the law, to write her a bill of divorcement, after which she was free to belong to some other man (Deut. 24:1-2). The New Testament takes exception to this: to divorce a woman and marry another, says Jesus, is to commit adultery (unless the divorce is on grounds of "fornication"), and a divorced woman who remarries commits adultery too, as does the fellow who marries her (Matt. 5:32; 19:9; Mark 10:11-12). "What therefore God hath joined together," says Christ, "let not man put asunder" (Mark 10:9).

The Old Testament in any case urges men to make the most of their marriages. "Rejoice with the wife of thy youth," says Proverbs, "and be thou ravished always with her love" (5:18-19). To the pessimistic author of Ecclesiastes, marriage helps make life worth living: "Live joyfully with the wife whom thou lovest all the days of the life of thy vanity" (9:9). The Hebrews, commanded to "be fruitful and multiply" (Gen. 1:28), also prized large families, hence the importance of a man staying married. Under the Hebrew levirate law (from *levir*, "brother-in-law"), a man was even obliged to marry his brother's widow if the brother died childless, to produce children in the brother's name (Deut. 25:5-10; see ONAN AND TAMAR and JUDAH AND TAMAR.)

Marriage is less important, and in fact discouraged by Paul as a worldly distraction, in the New Testament, due to the first Christians' view that the world is soon coming to an end. (See LOVEMAKING: TO KNOW IN THE BIBLICAL SENSE and PAUL: "BETTER TO MARRY THAN TO BURN.") Still, marriage is described as "honourable in all, and the bed undefiled" (Heb. 13:4). Husbands are told, "Love your wives" (Eph. 5:26), and wives, lest they forget their place, are told to "submit" (Col. 3:18) and "be in subjection" (1 Pet. 3:1), "for the husband is the head of the wife, even as Christ is the head of the church" (Eph. 5:23). Young wives, says Titus 2:4-5, should "be discreet, chaste, keepers at home, good, obedient to their own husbands, that the word of God be not blasphemed."

The Old Testament prophets portray the relationship between Yahweh and the Israelite people as that of husband and wife, but with Israel continually committing adultery, "a-whoring" after the Canaanite god Baal and other idols. Israel is not only divorced by Yahweh (Jer. 3:8) but violently punished for her unfaithfulness (see HOSEA, ISAIAH, JEREMIAH, and

EZEKIEL; on the issue of domestic violence in such passages, see YAHWEH). Yahweh promises, however, to take Israel back: "Thou shalt call me Ishi ('my man'), and shalt call me no more Baali ('my master')," says Yahweh in a play on words, "and I will betroth thee unto me for ever" (Hos. 2:16,19). In the New Testament, Christ upon his return is similarly to betroth, his bride being the church: "The marriage of the Lamb is come, and his wife hath made herself ready," and "Blessed are they which are called unto the marriage supper of the Lamb" (Rev. 19:7-9). (See also JERUSALEM: "AS A BRIDE ADORNED.")

MARY AND JOSEPH

See VIRGIN BIRTH: "CHILD OF THE HOLY GHOST."

MARY, CALLED MAGDALENE

Among Jesus Christ's followers, "ministering unto him," were "certain women" who "had been healed of evil spirits and infirmities" (Matt. 27:55; Luke 8:2). One of these women was "Mary called Magdalene" (that is, Mary of Magdala, a town in Galilee), out of whom Jesus "had cast seven devils" (Mark 16:9; Luke 8:2). Mary and "many other women" looked on from afar when Jesus was crucified (Matt . 27:55; Mark 15:40), she and "Mary the mother of James and Joses" sat by the sepulcher in which Jesus was entombed (Matt. 27:61), and the two Marys later brought spices to the sepulcher with the intention of anointing the body. It was to Mary Magdalene that Christ first appeared following his resurrection (Mark 16:9; John 20:1-18). Exclaiming "Rabboni!" ("Teacher!"), Mary embraced him, or tried to, prompting the risen Lord to tell her (in the original Greek of John's gospel), "me mou uptou" ("Do not cling to me" or "Do not hold on to me") (John 20:17).

It seems, based on the biblical text, that Mary Magdalene was an affectionate lady with some physical or psychological problems. But what did she do to get a bad reputation? The traditional view of her as a penitent whore seems to be literally a case of mistaken identity. There is no reason why Mary Magdalene should be identified with Luke's "woman in the city, which was a sinner"(7:37-50), John's "woman taken in adultery" (8:3-11), or anyone else. Nor should Mary be faulted for coming from Magdala, a reputedly wicked town, which may be why she left it. As for the "seven devils," demon possession was associated with sickness, not sin.

The fact is that demonizing as a sinner this woman who had been a leader among Jesus' disciples (at least after the top twelve males) fit the patriarchal agenda of the church in the late first century and afterward. Put in her place by a celibate male hierarchy, the penitent Mary, to quote Susan Haskins's excellent study of the Magdalene, "can stand as a metaphor for the historically subordinate position of women in Christianity." (See GENDER and PAUL.)

There is virtually nothing in the Bible to suggest that Mary Magdalene was Jesus' lover or wife (trying to embrace her "Teacher" hardly counts), though this is a notion found not just in fringe works such as *Holy Blood, Holy Grail* (summarized in Haskins). No less a body than the Jesus Seminar, an international group of biblical scholars formed in 1985, expresses the view that Jesus and the Magdalene probably had "a special relationship" (see Funk et al.). This seems to be based solely on the Seminar's view that the historical Jesus did not advocate celibacy. But what if Mary did?

The closest thing to real evidence of a "special relationship" between Mary and Jesus would seem to be an extrabiblical Gnostic work, the third-century Gospel of Philip, according to which Jesus loved "his companion" Mary more than all the other disciples, and often kissed her on the mouth, to the annoyance of the other disciples. (See also JESUS CHRIST).

⇒ PAUL

MASTURBATION/ONANISM

See ONAN AND TAMAR.

MENSTRUATION: Seven Lonely Days

"You shall be holy," Yahweh tells the children of Israel, "for the Lord your God is holy" (Lev. 17:2). In the so-called Holiness Code (Leviticus chapters 17-26), the Bible includes issues of semen and blood among things that for the Hebrews are "unclean," not in the sense of being dirty—see LOVEMAKING: TO KNOW IN THE BIBLICAL SENSE—but in the mysterious sense of being taboo, requiring ritual purification. Thus a man with an issue of semen and the woman with whom he has lain are to bathe in water and are "unclean till the evening" (Lev. 15:16-18). Purification takes longer, of course, for a menstruating woman. She is to be "put apart for her uncleanness" for seven days (Lev. 18:19). Any man who lies with her during this time is also unclean for seven days, anyone who touches her is unclean till the evening, and "everything that she sitteth upon shall be unclean" (Lev. 15:19-24).

Three well-known biblical women bear mentioning on the subject of menstruation. Bathsheba is either irresistible or else doesn't let on to King David, who makes love to her before she's through purifying (2 Sam. 11:4). In the apocryphal Additions to Esther, Queen Esther abhors her crown "like a menstrual rag" (14:16). And when Rachel in Genesis (31:19-35) steals her father Laban's household gods (*teraphim*), she comes up with a sure way of not getting caught: in her tent she hides the gods under a camel saddle and sits on it. When Laban comes hunting for the figurines, Rachel apologizes for not getting up, saying, "The custom of women is upon me." Laban doesn't dare touch either her or the saddle, and thus doesn't find his gods.

To the prophet Ezekiel, going near a woman who is menstruating is just as bad as committing adultery or idolatry (18:5).

(Ezekiel doesn't like women, period. See EZEKIEL.) Yet Jesus, when a woman who suffers from a twelve-year "flow of blood" touches his garment, stops to speak with and heal her (Matt. 9:20-22; Mark 5:24-34; Luke 8:43-48).

METHUSELAH: You're Never Too Old

The oldest man in the Bible is Noah's grandfather Methuselah, who lived for nine hundred and sixty-nine years. Methuselah is eighth in the ten-man Sethite genealogy, a list of who begat whom from Adam's third son Seth down to Noah, who was six hundred years old at the time of the Flood. (The average number of years lived in the Sethite genealogy is seven hundred and sixty-five years—though Enoch, whom God called home alive after only three hundred and sixty-five years, shouldn't count.)

Methuselah was a relatively young one hundred and eighty-seven when he begat his first son Lamech. Methuselah "begat (other) sons and daughters," though we don't know if he quickened his pace in begetting. If Methuselah fathered only one child every one hundred and eighty-seven years, he would have five kids, with one more on the way, before he died, we may assume of old age.   (GEN. 5:25-27)

⇒ LAMECH, THE WORLD'S FIRST POLYGAMIST

MICHAL AND DAVID

See DAVID AND MICHAL.

MISOGYNY: "Adam Was Not Deceived"

See GENDER: "MALE AND FEMALE CREATED HE THEM" *and* PAUL: "BETTER TO MARRY THAN TO BURN."

MOAB, THE DAUGHTERS OF

See COZBI AND ZIMRI *and* RUTH: "AT HIS FEET UNTIL MORNING."

MOSES AND ZIPPORAH

Moses first meets Zipporah at a Midianite well—an auspicious beginning, as love blossoms at biblical wells (see ISAAC AND REBEKAH and JACOB AND LABAN'S DAUGHTERS). Wanted for murder in Egypt, the fugitive Moses happens to be sitting by the well when Zipporah and her six sisters come to water their father's flock. When shepherds run these maidens off, Moses rises to the women's defense and helps them water their animals.

Zipporah's father Jethro (also called Reuel), gratefully taking Moses in, gives the Hebrew both a job (as a shepherd) and Zipporah to marry. She bears Moses two sons, Gershom and Eliezer, still children when Yahweh calls Moses to go back to Egypt and tell the Pharoah to "let my people go." (On the Hebrew problem in Egypt, see ISRAEL.)

On Moses' way to Egypt there occurs one of the most mysterious episodes in the Bible. Yahweh, for some reason, tries to kill Moses, and it is Zipporah who comes to the rescue: with a sharp stone she circumcises "her son"—which one is not specified—and holds the severed foreskin to Moses' genitals (euphemistically called "feet") while saying, "Surely a bloody husband art thou to me." As a result, Yahweh spares Moses, with Zipporah reiterating, "A bloody husband thou art, because of the circumcision."

Scholars today can only guess at the meaning of this primitive passage. Is Yahweh angry enough to kill because Moses—raised as an Egyptian—is uncircumcised, and does Zipporah therefore circumcise Moses vicariously? (See CIRCUMCISION:

"SIGN OF THE COVENANT.") In any case Moses, thanks to Zipporah, escapes by the skin of his feet to fulfill his biblical mission.

Zipporah and her sons live with Jethro while Moses leads his people out of Egypt, then they rejoin Moses in the desert. But after that Zipporah is not mentioned again—unless complaints by Moses' brother Aaron and sister Miriam about his "Cushite woman" (RSV, NRSV) refer to Zipporah (Numbers 12). "Cushite" in its broad sense would include "Midianite"; only in its narrow sense does it mean "Ethiopian" (KJV). (If Moses has a black wife, and if that is why Miriam complains, there is irony in the way Miriam is punished by Yahweh: her skin is turned a leprous snow-white.)

Zipporah may be the Bible's most underrated woman. Were it not for the Midianite lady's swift action, saving the life of her husband Moses, the Pharoah might *never* have let those people go.

(EX. 2:11-22; 4:19-26; 18:1-6)   ⇒ AARON AND THE GOLDEN CALF

N

NAKEDNESS/NUDITY

See GENITALS: "THEY KNEW THAT THEY WERE NAKED."

NEHEMIAH: "Cleansed I Them of All Strangers"

See EZRA: "YE HAVE TAKEN STRANGE WIVES."

NEPHILIM, BIRTH OF THE

See SONS OF GOD: "THEY TOOK THEM WIVES."

NOAH: Unsunk, and Drunk as a Skunk

When Yahweh sees that "every imagination" of man's heart is "only evil continually," he regrets having created man and decides to "destroy all flesh" with a flood. A six-hundred-year-old fellow named Noah, however, finds "favor in the eyes of the Lord," and survives the deluge with his wife, three sons and their spouses, and pairs of all "kinds" of animals, by building an ark according to Yahweh's instructions.

The Bible doesn't say what prevents so many animals from

reproducing and overpopulating the ark during its long voyage. According to later Jewish tradition, Noah simply prohibits the critters from having sex, and prohibits his sons Shem, Ham, and Japheth from having sex with their wives. Tradition says also that Ham, the dog, and the cock-raven disobey Noah and have sex anyway. (See Graves and Patai's *Hebrew Myths*).

Once back on dry land, Noah's sons and their wives begin the task of repopulating the earth. Meanwhile Noah goes into farming. Planting a vineyard, he winds up getting shellacked on the wine and lies naked in his tent. His youngest son Ham, seeing Noah in this condition, informs brothers Shem and Japheth outside.

To avoid seeing their father's nakedness, Shem and Japheth enter the tent walking backwards and, keeping their faces turned away, cover Noah with a garment.

When Noah awakes and learns "what his youngest son had done to him," he utters a seemingly confused condemnation. "Cursed be Canaan," Noah says, "a slave of slaves shall he be to his brothers." But what does this mean? It was Ham, not Ham's son Canaan, who was unfortunate enough to see Noah's nakedness, yet it's Canaan—progenitor of the inhabitants of the land that the Hebrews will later invade—who gets cursed.

The phrase "what his youngest son had done to him" implies something more than mere looking, though nothing else now remains in the text. Perhaps, as Steven L. McKenzie suggests, Ham's offense was disrespect, in failing to cover Noah's nakedness. (See GENITALS: "THEY KNEW THAT THEY WERE NAKED.") In legendary versions (see Graves and Patai), Ham or Canaan emasculates Noah, certainly stronger grounds for a curse. In any case, the wrong person in Genesis gets cursed, the obvious intent of the biblical scribes being to justify the Israelite conquest of Canaan (already history when this story is told), with the added implication that the Canaanites deserved it for their sexual perversions (see the list in Lev. 18:1-25).

A Dead Sea Scroll called the Genesis Florilegium at least offers an excuse for Noah's cursing of Canaan: Noah could not curse Ham because God had already blessed Noah's sons (Gen.

9:1). (A more Freudian excuse for the curse: Noah resented
Canaan for having been conceived on the ark despite Noah's
ban on sex.) But the injustice of cursing Ham's son seems
acknowledged in the pseudepigraphical book of Jubilees (called
also "The Little Genesis"): Ham, finding Noah's curse upon
Canaan "disgusting," takes Canaan and his other sons and
separates from his father.   (GEN. 9:20-27; JUB. 7:13)

⇒ SHEM, FIRST OF THE SEMITES

O

OHOLAH AND OHOLIBAH

See EZEKIEL: TALKING LEWD WOMEN.

ONAN AND TAMAR

The Hebrew patriarch Jacob has a grandson named Er who is so prone to err (he is "wicked in the sight of the Lord") that God slays him. This leaves Er's widow Tamar with no children. But Er has two brothers, Onan and Shelah, which sets the stage for a levirate marriage, according to which a man would marry a childless brother's widow in order to give the dead brother offspring (Deut. 25:5-10).

"Go in unto thy brother's wife," Er's father Judah dutifully tells his second son Onan, "and marry her, and raise up seed to thy brother."

Onan doesn't like the idea that any child he gives Er's widow Tamar will not be his own. So he tries to get around his obligation: when Onan, we are told, "went in unto his brother's wife, he spilled (the semen) on the ground."

These boys of Judah really try the Lord's patience: Yahweh now slays Onan too. Historically some have tried to see this as a condemnation of masturbation, with Onan's sin even named after him. But onanism in the sense of masturbation for self-gratification is not what is involved here. (No such act is mentioned in the Bible, unless one so interprets Ezek. 16:17, in which the harlot Jerusalem made for herself "images of men, and didst commit whoredom with them," or, as suggested by Gerald Larue, Matt. 5:30, "If thy right hand offend thee, cut it off.") Whether Onan masturbates or, more in context, performs coitus interruptus, his intent is to avoid impregnating Tamar "lest that he should give seed to his brother." Onan's sin is thus one of omission, specifically non-fulfillment of the levirate law.

Er still has one brother left, but Judah has to wonder if trying to impregnate Tamar is worth risking a third son's life. For Tamar's own answer to the problem, see JUDAH AND TAMAR.

(GENESIS 38)

P

PATRIARCHY: "He Shall Rule over Thee"

See GENDER: "MALE AND FEMALE CREATED HE THEM."

PAUL: "Better to Marry than to Burn"

According to the Apostle Paul, we "all have sinned and come short of the glory of God" (Rom. 3:23) ("I am carnal, sold under sin," and "O wretched man that I am!" are two of Paul's ascetic self-descriptions [Rom. 7:14,24]); "we are justified freely by (God's) grace through the redemption that is in Christ Jesus" (Rom. 3:24), there being "neither Jew nor Greek, . . . male nor female," for we are all one in Christ; and "the time is short," "the fashion of this world is passing away" (1 Cor. 7:29,31), as the return of Christ is imminent (cf. Matt. 16:28; James 5:8-9).

It is in this context of a sinful world soon ending that Paul agrees with the Corinthians that "it is good for a man not to touch a woman" (1 Cor. 7:1). He apparently does not mean to denigrate women—Paul could just as easily say (were it not for the patriarchal mind-set of his day), "It is good for a woman not to touch a man." He is counseling Christians of both sexes who are unmarried to remain so, and thus to be celibate, as Paul has chosen to be; for those who are married "careth for the things of the world," such as how to please one's mate, when one should be caring instead, given the shortness of time, about "how he may please the Lord" (1 Cor. 7:32-34). "I have espoused you to one husband," Paul tells the Corinthians meta-phorically, "that I may present you as a chaste virgin to Christ" (2 Cor. 11:2). The passing of this world is why Paul expresses no interest in procreation, so highly valued by his Hebrew fore-bears. But if a man and a woman, for the short time left, cannot contain their sexual desire, "let them marry," says Paul, "for it is better to marry than to burn" (1 Cor. 7:9). He also counsels married couples to "come together" regularly, except for any agreed periodic abstentions, to avoid extramarital temptation (1 Cor. 7:2-5). As for what Paul considers illicit sex, such as homosexuality and any sex outside of marriage, he condemns such "fornication" irrespective of time frame (see FORNICATION: "GOING AFTER STRANGE FLESH").

But considering Paul's discouragement of marriage in his words to the Corinthians and Romans, what should we make of the later letters to Timothy and Titus, in which marriage and procreation are encouraged? "I will therefore that the younger women marry," says 1 Tim. 5:14, "bear children, guide the house." What had happened in the interim to cause such a reversal of position?

More to the point is what had *not* happened, namely the end of the world. Scholars suspect, based on style as well as content, that Paul's words to Timothy and Titus are not Paul's words at all, but those of someone writing in his name, years after Paul's death, and with an oppressive agenda toward women. Specific-ally, with the *Parousia* (Christ's second coming) seemingly post-poned indefinitely, it was time to get women out of leadership roles in the church. Women prominent in the church of Paul's day included Lydia, Priscilla, Phoebe, Junia, Tryphena and Tryphosa (Acts 16:14-15; Rom. 16:1,3,12). But patriarchy was the world's social norm, and, as the years wore on, conformity, so male church leaders said, would keep Christians out of trouble—giving "(no) occasion to the adversary to speak reproachfully" of the Christian community (1 Tim. 5:16).

This meant putting women in their culturally perceived place, which the church proceeded to do. Thus women, accord-ing to the letter to Titus, are to be "keepers at home" and "obedient" to their husbands, "that the word of God be not blasphemed" (2:5). "Let the women learn in silence with all subjection," says 1 Tim. 2:11, for "I suffer not a woman to teach, nor to usurp authority over the man." This was reinforced by what appears to be an addition, out of character with the rest of Paul's text, to 1 Corinthians (14:34): "Let your women keep silence in the churches." Nor was this subordination just a matter of worldly custom, for 1 Tim. 2:13-14 would have us know that Adam, not Eve, was formed first in Genesis, and that it was the woman, not the man, who was deceived and "was in transgression." (See GENDER.)

This is Paul the woman hater, as though the earlier Paul's statement that there is "neither male nor female" in Christ was some kind of mistake, or has in any case become inoperative. And it is this later "Paul," with help from Augustine (354-430 C.E.) and other church fathers, who saddled Christianity with misogynistic baggage that it still totes today.   ⇒ BABYLON

POLYGAMY/POLYGYNY

See CONCUBINES: "MANY STRANGE WOMEN" *and* MARRIAGE: "THEY SHALL BE ONE FLESH."

PROCREATION: "Give Me Children, or Else I Die"

See CONCEPTION: "MADE IN SECRET" *and* LOVEMAKING: TO KNOW IN THE BIBLICAL SENSE.

PRODIGAL SON, THE

"By means of a whorish woman," warns Proverbs (6:26), "a man is brought to a piece of bread." In Jesus' parable of the Prodigal

Son, a young man is brought to less than that: his father's servants have "bread enough" while he's starving to death, in a far-off land where he has whored away the inheritance that he requested and received from his father, and where there now is a famine. He is reduced to a job feeding swine—unclean animals under Jewish law (Lev. 11:7, Deut. 14:8)—and is hungry enough to eat the pigs' slop himself.

This sad victim of "riotous living" finally decides to head home. His father, seeing him from afar, runs to meet him with a hug and a kiss. "Father, I have sinned against heaven, and in thy sight," says the repentant lad, "and am no more worthy to be called thy son." But the joyous father, saying "Let us eat, and be merry," orders the killing of a fatted calf, and has his servants fetch his son some fine clothes.

When the elder son in this family comes home from the field to find "music and dancing," and is told it's because "Thy brother is come," he is so angry he will not go in. "Lo, these many years do I serve thee," with every order obeyed, he bitterly tells his father outside, "yet thou never gavest me a kid, that I might make merry with my friends," but as soon as this other son comes home, who "hath devoured thy living with harlots, thou hast killed for him the fatted calf."

"Son," the father explains to him, "thou art ever with me, and all that I have is thine." But "we should make merry, and be glad: for this thy brother was dead, and is alive again; and was lost, and is found." (See also HARLOTRY: "A-WHORING AFTER OTHER GODS.")   (LUKE 15:11-32)

PROSTITUTION: Is Nothing Sacred?

Prostitution in ancient Hebrew society was morally censured but was not illegal. "Do not prostitute thy daughter," says Yahweh in Lev. 19:29, "to cause her to be a whore" (*zonah*, the Hebrew word for a prostitute or loose woman). Yahweh prohibits Israelite priests from marrying whores (Lev. 21:7), and notes that among Israel's moral "transgressions" a man and his father "go in unto" the same woman (presumably a prostitute) (Amos 2:7). Yahweh lists among the deeds for which he will judge the nations the trading of "a boy for a harlot" (Joel 3:3). Yet a *zonah* herself, if single, is guilty of no biblical crime (unless she's a priest's daughter, in which case, says Lev. 21:9, she "profaneth her father" and "shall be burnt with fire").

Legal prostitution in the Bible reflects the old double standard at work. While his wife must be faithful, a Hebrew man can consort with an unmarried prostitute and not be guilty of adultery. But if the whore's a wife too—virtually another man's property under the patriarchal system of the Hebrews—then both she and her customer are adulterers, a crime for which the penalty is death (Lev. 20:10; Deut. 22:22).

Until recent years it was the conventional wisdom that cultic sex or sacred prostitution took place in Israel and elsewhere in the ancient Near East. It is certainly true that the Bible makes extensive use of adultery, whoring, and other sexual metaphors to describe the children of Israel's unfaithfulness to Yahweh (see ADULTERY and HARLOTRY.) But metaphors are figures of speech. Many biblical scholars now point to a lack of textual or any other kind of evidence for the practice of sacred prostitution. Tikva Frymer-Kensky calls the whole idea "a myth" based on "ancient and modern sexual fantasies."

Central to the issue is the significance of the word *qedeshim* and its related forms. In Israel, in addition to the all-male priests, there were male cultic functionaries called *qedeshim* ("holy men") and female ones called *qedeshot* ("holy women"). Their only biblically stated activity is found in 2 Kings 23:7: "The women (*qedeshot*) wove hangings for the grove" (see ASHE-RAH). Yet translators and commentators have traditionally called these functionaries cult prostitutes. A key passage is Deut. 23:17, in which these personnel are outlawed: "There shall be no *qedeshah* ('holy woman') among the daughters of Israel and no *qadesh* ('holy man') among the sons of Israel." This verse is immediately followed by: "You shall not bring the wages of a prostitute (*zonah*), or the price of a dog (*keleb*) into the house of Yahweh your God." But it is not clear, from the juxtaposition of these two verses, that *qedeshah* ("holy woman") and *zonah* ("prostitute") are being equated, or that the *qedeshim* are being referred to as dogs. (On other problematic passages, see JUDAH AND TAMAR and COZBI AND ZIMRI.)

It is known from the Ugaritic texts that the Canaanite cult (predating the Hebrew) also included holy men (duties unknown) called *qedeshim*. Perhaps a desire to rid the Hebrew cult of any vestige of Canaanite influence led to the Deuteronomic law against these functionaries. Thus King Josiah, in addition to destroying Baalim altars and cutting down groves, "broke down the houses of the *qedeshim* that were by the house of the Lord" (2 Kings 23:7). King Asa similarly "took the *qedeshim* out of the land" (1 Kings 15:12). But whatever the *qedeshim* were, Frymer-Kensky and others consider it presumptuous to translate the term as "cult prostitutes" (RSV) or, as the KJV renders it, "sodomites" (1 Kings 14:24, 22:46, 2 Kings 23:7). Carol Yee suggests that a better translation of *qedeshah*, etc., in the absence of more information, would be "hierodule" (as used also by Theodor Gaster in editing Frazer's *The New Golden Bough*, and by Phyllis Bird), which simply means "temple servant."

PROVERBS, THE BOOK OF

See ADULTERY: FIRE IN THE BOSOM; HARLOTRY: "A-WHORING AFTER OTHER GODS"; *and* YAHWEH: "THY MAKER IS THINE HUSBAND."

PURITY, RITUAL

See LOVEMAKING: TO KNOW IN THE BIBLICAL SENSE *and* MENSTRUATION: SEVEN LONELY DAYS.

Q

QEDESHIM/QEDESHOTH

See PROSTITUTION: IS NOTHING SACRED?

QUEEN OF HEAVEN

See BAALIM AND ASHTAROTH.

QUEEN OF SHEBA

See SOLOMON AND HIS "OUTLANDISH WOMEN."

R

RACHEL AND JACOB

See JACOB AND LABAN'S DAUGHTERS.

RAHAB THE HARLOT

When Moses dies atop Mount Nebo in Moab, overlooking the Canaanite city of Jericho across the Jordan River, Joshua becomes the leader of the children of Israel. Preparing to invade Canaan, Joshua sends two spies across the Jordan, telling them, "Go, view the land, even Jericho."

Slipping into Jericho, the spies go to see a harlot named Rahab. We are not told if this is according to instructions, or if the spies go to a harlot's house because they have just spent several years in the wilderness. In any case they are not very good spies, for the king of Jericho is told that the two Hebrews are lodging with Rahab, whose house is in the wall of the city. (Perhaps the spies have gone to Rahab's for the excellent view.)

The king sends men to the harlot's house, but Rahab, on being told that her two guests are Hebrew spies, tells the king's men that the two just departed, as it is dark and time to shut the city gate. Hurry after them, Rahab says, and "ye shall overtake them."

Rushing out the city gate, the king's men head for the Jordan in pursuit, so they think, of the spies. Meanwhile Rahab joins the two spies on her roof, where she has hidden them under some flax.

"I know that the Lord hath given you the land," she tells the Hebrews, based on what she has heard about the parting of the Red Sea and all. "Your terror is fallen upon us," and "the Lord your God, he is God in heaven above, and in earth beneath." Rahab asks that, in exchange for the help she has given, the Hebrew invaders "save alive my father, and my mother, and my brethren, and my sisters, and all that they have." (Another mystery about Rahab is why, with all those family ties, she is a prostitute.)

"Our life for yours," the two spies assure her, "if ye utter not this our business." Rahab lets them down the wall by a cord through the window, and they escape, after telling her to tie a scarlet ribbon in the window, and to bring all her kin into the house when the invasion begins.

Terror indeed falls: the Hebrew invaders, imposing the ban or *herem*, kill every living thing in Jericho, except for Rahab and her family, who are spared as the Hebrews promised.

Rahab lives in Israel "even unto this day," says the book of Joshua. At some point, as the Hebrew conquest of the land of Canaan proceeds, Rahab marries a man named Salmon, by whom she has a son named Boaz, the future husband of Ruth (Matt. 1:5).

In the New Testament, Rahab is held up as an example of what both works and faith can do. "Was not Rahab the harlot justified by works?" asks the Letter of James rhetorically (2:25). Also "by faith," says Hebrews (11:31), "the harlot Rahab perished not with them that believed not, when she had received the spies with peace."   (JOSH. 2:1-21; 6:17,21-25)   ⇒ GIDEON

RAPE: "Lewdness and Folly in Israel"

Sexual intercourse with another man's wife was adultery under Hebrew law, a violation of the seventh commandment (Ex. 20:14; Deut. 5:18) punishable by death for the adulterers (Lev. 20:10; Deut. 22:22). Presumably the wife would be executed only if she consented to the sexual encounter, though in the text itself no distinction is made between rape and consent of a married woman.

With regard to the rape of a virgin, the fate of the rapist depended on whether or not the virgin was betrothed to another man at the time. If betrothed, she was considered to belong to her future husband, in which case the rapist faced death (Deut. 22:23). If the damsel was not betrothed, the rapist was required to marry her, paying her father the bride price or *mohar* of fifty shekels of silver, and could not divorce her "all his days" (Deut. 22:28-29).

The only proof of rape scripturally provided for is the betrothed virgin screaming for help. If the sexual incident occurred in the city, where someone presumably could hear the virgin scream but no one did, she was assumed to be guilty of consent and would die along with the man (Deut. 22:23-24). The virgin would be spared if the incident occurred "in the field," where she may have screamed but "there was none to save her" (Deut. 22:25-26).

One of the Bible's most horrific episodes is the gang rape in Gibeah of the Levite's concubine (Judg. 19:1-30). ("Lewdness and folly in Israel," as the Levite describes it, hardly captures the horror of the incident, not to mention what the Levite does afterwards. See BENJAMIN.) An intended homosexual gang rape in Sodom precedes Yahweh's destruction of the city, the intended rape victims being none other than angels of the Lord (Gen. 19:1-25; see SODOM[Y] AND GOMORRAH).

King David's son Amnon is assassinated by order of Amnon's half-brother Absalom for raping David's daughter Tamar (2 Sam. 13:1-29; see AMNON AND TAMAR). The Hivite prince Shechem rapes Dinah, Jacob's daughter by Leah, for which Jacob's sons exact vengeance (Genesis 34; see SHECHEM AND DINAH). According to the pseudepigraphical Testament of Reuben, Reuben's sexual intercourse with his father's concubine Bilhah (Gen. 35:22) was rape: Bilhah was passed-out drunk at the time.

Rape in some biblical passages is seen as a form of divine punishment. Thus the Babylonians, instruments of Yahweh's wrath, "ravished the women in Zion, and the maids in the cities of Judah" (Lam. 5:22). Later the Babylonians, in turn, see "their wives ravished" by Yahweh's instruments the Medes (Isa. 13:16-17). Yahweh himself is described as a defiler of women. "Therefore will I discover thy skirts upon thy face," Yahweh tells the inhabitants of Judah, "that thy shame may appear" (Jer. 13:26). He likewise tells Nineveh that he will lift her skirts over her face and show "the nations (her) nakedness, and the kingdoms (her) shame" (Nahum 3:5), and in Isaiah Yahweh rapes the "virgin daughter of Babylon" (47:1-4). "The Lord will discover their secret parts," says Isaiah of the daughters of Zion (3:17), and Yahweh in the book of Lamentations "hath trodden the virgin, the daughter of Judah, as in a winepress" (1:15). Needless to say, these are problematic passages for women readers of the Bible, and for theologians of either gender. (See YAHWEH: "THY MAKER IS THINE HUSBAND.")

REBEKAH: "Neither Had Any Man Known Her"

See ISAAC AND REBEKAH.

REHOBOAM: Seventy-Eight Wives and Concubines

See MAACHAH AND REHOBOAM.

REPRODUCTION: "Be Fruitful and Multiply"

See CONCEPTION: "MADE IN SECRET" *and* LOVEMAKING: TO KNOW IN THE BIBLICAL SENSE.

REUBEN AND BILHAH

See JACOB AND LABAN'S DAUGHTERS *and* RAPE: "LEWD-
NESS AND FOLLY IN ISRAEL."

REVELATION, THE BOOK OF

See BABYLON, "THE MOTHER OF HARLOTS"; JERUSA-
LEM: "AS A BRIDE ADORNED"; *and* VIRGINITY: "THE
BRIDEGROOM REJOICETH."

RUTH: "At His Feet Until Morning"

In the book of Ruth, set in the time of the judges, a rich man of
Bethlehem named Boaz, full of food and drink after barley
harvest, lies down to sleep by the heap of grain on his threshing
floor. At midnight he awakes with a start, and finds a woman
lying at his "feet" (a euphemism for his sexual organs), which
the woman has uncovered.

"Who art thou?" Boaz asks, not recognizing the woman in
the dark.

"I am Ruth thine handmaid," she replies.

Ruth is the young Moabite widow of a late kinsman of Boaz.
She and Boaz first met when Ruth was gleaning grain (as the
poor are allowed to do) left behind by harvesters, in what
happened to be Boaz's field. On learning who she was, Boaz had
instructed his men to see that some grain was left for her, and
to allow Ruth to glean "even among the sheaves" without
reproach. Now her mother-in-law Naomi, a widow herself, has
put Ruth up to coming by night to the threshing floor—"uncover his feet, and lay thee down"—as a bold way for Ruth to
propose.

"Spread therefore thy skirt over thine handmaid," Ruth

tells Boaz, "for thou art a near kinsman." To spread his skirt over her would signify taking possession (cf. Ezek. 16:8), and the term "near kinsman" translates the Hebrew word *go'el* ("redeemer")—a man who protects the heritage of a deceased relative by buying his property, and perhaps by marrying his widow, as in levirate marriage (see MARRIAGE).

Whether sexual intercourse takes place on the threshing floor is not stated, though Ruth's action and words seem an open invitation. Boaz in any case has her stay all night; Ruth lies "at his feet until morning," though she leaves before it's light enough for people to recognize each other. Apparently eager to accept her proposal, Boaz must first see if a nearer kinsman, whom the book does not name, will waive his right to redeem the property involved, Ruth included.

The nearer kinsman indeed waives his right, and Boaz marries Ruth. When Boaz "went in unto her," we are told, "the Lord gave her conception." Ruth bears a son named Obed.

Ruth is admired as one of the Bible's most resourceful women. (She also shows exemplary loyalty. "Whither thou goest," she tells Naomi, returning from Moab to Judah, "I will go.") Ruth overcomes the fact that she is a Moabite female in Hebrew patriarchal society. ("No Ammonite or Moabite," says Deut. 23:3, "shall enter the assembly of God.") The rich Boaz seems also to have beaten the odds, being the son of a Canaanite prostitute (Matt. 1:5; see RAHAB THE HARLOT). Ruth and Boaz are King David's great-grandparents. (RUTH) ⇒ HANNAH

S

SALOME: "Even Half of My Kingdom"

See HEROD AND THE DANCE OF SALOME.

SAMARIA: "Hot as an Oven"

"The wickedness of Samaria," capital city of the kingdom of Israel, is "her rebellion against God," which will lead to the city's destruction. So declares the prophet Hosea (7:1, 13:16), who identifies that rebellion metaphorically as sexual profligacy. "They are all adulterers," Hosea says of Israel and Samaria, "hot as an oven" (7:4,7). Things get even hotter in Ezekiel 23,, which casts Samaria as one of two lewd sisters (the other being Jerusalem), both wives of Yahweh, who commit adultery with Assyrians, Egyptians, and others. For this Yahweh delivers her "into the hands of her lovers" the Assyrians, who in fact destroy Samaria and the kingdom of Israel in 722 B.C.E.

The destruction is graphically foretold by Hosea. The people of Samaria "shall fall by the sword: their infants shall be dashed in pieces, and their women with child shall be ripped up" (13.16). Yahweh "will come down," says the prophet Micah, and make Samaria "a heap in the field," and will smash and burn with fire all the idols she has gathered with her harlot's wages (1:6-7). (See also ISRAEL.)

139

SAMSON AND DELILAH

In the time of the judges the angel of the Lord announces to Manoah the Danite and his barren wife that the latter will conceive and bear a son. The child is to be consecrated as a Nazarite, whose vows include no strong drink or haircuts.

Manoah's wife conceives and bears Samson, the son who according to the angel "shall begin to deliver Israel from the hand of the Philistines." But on growing up, Samson, though blessed by the Lord with great physical strength, spends more time consorting with the Philistines than delivering Israelites from them. For starters, he falls for and marries a Philistine woman, and entertains thirty Philistine companions at a seven-day wedding feast. Unfortunately the father of the bride gives the bride to Samson's best man when the father assumes (wrongly) that Samson has spurned her. The father offers Samson a substitute ("Is not her younger sister fairer than she?"), but Samson—already mad at the wedding guests for having manipulated his wife in the solving of a riddle (they had "plowed with [his] heifer," to use Samson's sexist phrase)—is now so angry that he burns the Philistines' cornfields and vineyards.

The Philistines retaliate by burning up Samson's best man's wife and father-in-law. Vowing to get them for that, Samson smites the Philistines "hip and thigh with a great slaughter."

Samson next sees a harlot in the Philistine town of Gaza and, as Judges describes it, he "went in unto her." That night while he's with her, the Philistines, planning to nab him in the morning, surround the area and hide in the gate of the city. But at midnight Samson arises, puts the doors, posts, and bar of the gate on his shoulders, and totes the whole works to the top of a hill. It is unclear whether Samson does this to impress his date or to thwart the hiding Philistines after somehow becoming aware of their presence.

Samson next loves Delilah, "a woman in the valley of Sorek." Delilah may or may not be a Philistine, but the Philistines use her against Samson. "Entice him," the lords of the

Philistines tell her, "and see wherein his great strength lieth, and by what means we may prevail against him, . . . and we will give thee every one of us eleven hundred pieces of silver."

At the first good opportunity, Delilah asks Samson, "Tell me, I pray thee, wherein thy great strength lieth, and wherewith thou mightest be bound to afflict thee." Samson tells her that if he is bound with seven green bowstrings that have not been dried, he will be as weak as any other man.

In what might be interpreted as a kinky sex game (Samson not suspecting her true motive), Delilah binds Samson with the appropriate bowstrings, which she obtains from the Philistine lords. Then, with men lying in wait in the chamber, Delilah says, "The Philistines be upon thee, Samson." Samson snaps the bowstrings, again frustrating his would-be captors.

On two more occasions Delilah, accusing Samson of mocking her, asks him wherein his strength lies and how he might be bound. Both times she tries what he tells her ("The Philistines be upon thee, Samson"), and each time it turns out he has lied.

Delilah now really goes to work on him. "How canst thou say, I love thee, when thine heart is not with me?" she pouts. "Thou hast mocked me these three times, and hast not told me wherein thy great strength lieth." She presses him daily till Samson is "vexed unto death" and finally tells her the truth: he has been a Nazarite from birth, a razor never having touched his head: "If I be shaven, then my strength will go from me, and I shall become weak, and be like any other man."

Delilah sees that he speaks from the heart, and sends for the Philistine lords, who come with "money in their hand." While Samson lies asleep on her knees, Delilah has a man "shave off the seven locks of his head." Again it's "The Philistines be upon thee, Samson," and this time, as Samson awakes, the Philistines indeed are upon him. His strength gone, Samson is taken away, his eyes are gouged out, and he is put to work grinding corn in the prison house.

But the Philistines forget to keep giving him haircuts. One day as he is displayed for sport in the crowd-filled temple of Dagon, with the lords of the Philistines present, Samson literally

brings down the house: he has gained enough strength from his growing hair to dislodge the temple's two middle pillars. His last words are "Let me die with the Philistines," and he dies with over three thousand of them as the building collapses. Contrary to Cecil B. DeMille's Hollywood epic, we are not told if Delilah (repentant in the movie) is anywhere around at the time.
(JUDGES 13-16)   ⇒ BENJAMIN

SARAH AND TOBIAS

An Israelite exile named Raguel lives with his wife and daughter in the Median capital of Ecbatana following the Assyrian destruction of Israel in 722 B.C.E. Raguel's daughter Sarah has a hard time keeping a husband. In fact she's had seven in a row, and not one of them has survived the first night with her. Each bridegroom has been killed by Asmodeus ("destroyer"), a demon in love with Sarah, before the marriage could be consummated. Her father's maids reproach Sarah, even accuse her of strangling all her husbands. She contemplates hanging herself, and prays to God for either death or an end to this torment.

God hears her prayer, and sends the angel Raphael to resolve both Sarah's problem and that of an Israelite named Tobit, among exiles in the Assyrian capital of Nineveh. Tobit is blind, having gotten bird droppings in his eyes, and is reproached by Anna his wife. Like Sarah in Ecbatana, Tobit in Nineveh has prayed to God for death.

Not wanting to leave his family in poverty, Tobit sends his son Tobias to the Median town of Rages, to get some money that Tobit left in trust there years earlier. A man who calls himself Azarias is hired to go with Tobias. Little do Tobit and Tobias know that the man is actually the angel Raphael.

On the way to Media, Tobias, on Raphael's instructions, catches a fish, which they cook and eat after removing and keeping the heart, liver, and gall. At Ecbatana the angel informs Tobias that they will stay with a cousin of Tobit's named Raguel.

This Raguel, he adds, has an only daughter, of whom Tobias is the only eligible kinsman, and Raphael will suggest to Raguel that Tobias marry her.

Tobias knows all about Raguel's daughter, and expresses to Raphael his fear of being the next husband to die in her bridal chamber. But Raphael tells Tobias what to do to rid Sarah of her jealous demon-lover. With that knowledge, Tobias is in love with her even before Sarah greets them at her father's door.

When a marriage is proposed over supper, Raguel tells Tobias, "Eat, drink, and be merry, for you have a right to take my child," but Raguel then warns him about Sarah's dead husbands. When Tobias refuses to eat till they have a binding agreement on the matter, Raguel says, "Take her right now."

A marriage contract is signed, they eat, then the bridal chamber is prepared, and there Sarah is taken to wait. Sarah fearfully weeps, but when Tobias enters the chamber, he knows just what to do. He burns the fish heart and liver on incense coals, creating a foul-smelling smoke. It so repels the demon Asmodeus that he flees to the farthest parts of Egypt, where Raphael binds him. Tobias and Sarah, after praying that they grow old together, now consummate their marriage.

Raguel sends a maid into the chamber to see if the man's still alive. She reports back that the couple is asleep. Raguel, giving thanks to God, sends servants out to fill in a grave that he had already dug for Tobias.

The jubilant Raguel now hosts a fourteen-day wedding feast, with Tobias of course obliged to attend, while Tobias's parents back home are wondering what has become of him.

When Tobias finally comes home with Sarah, he uses the fish gall, as Raphael has instructed him, to restore his father Tobit's sight.   (APOCRYPHA: TOBIT)   ⇒ JEREMIAH

SARAH, WIFE OF ABRAHAM

See ABRAHAM AND SARAH.

SEXUAL INTERCOURSE

See LOVEMAKING: TO KNOW IN THE BIBLICAL SENSE.

SEXUAL ORGANS

See BREASTS: "MILK OUT, AND BE DELIGHTED" *and* GEN-
ITALS: "THEY KNEW THAT THEY WERE NAKED."

SEXUAL SINS

See ADULTERY: "FIRE IN THE BOSOM"; BESTIALITY: NO
FIT HELPER; FORNICATION: "GOING AFTER STRANGE
FLESH"; HARLOTRY: "A-WHORING AFTER OTHER
GODS"; HOMOSEXUALITY: "THAT WHICH IS UNSEEMLY";
INCEST: "COME LIE WITH ME, MY SISTER"; LESBIANISM:
"AGAINST NATURE"; RAPE: "LEWDNESS AND FOLLY IN
ISRAEL"; *and* SODOM(Y) AND GOMORRAH.

SHECHEM AND DINAH

When Dinah, daughter of the Hebrew patriarch Jacob, goes out
with some Canaanite girlfriends, she catches the eye of a Canaanite (specifically Hivite) prince named Shechem. The prince
rapes Dinah: we are told that Shechem "took her, and lay with
her, and defiled her." Afterwards, however, Shechem loves
Dinah, treats her kindly, and asks his father Hamor, "Get me
this damsel to wife." Dinah, moreover, does not go home but
stays in the prince's house. Does she do this willingly? Does
Dinah return Shechem's love? There is no way to know, for the
story of Shechem and Dinah is a perfect example of the an-

drocentrism or male-centeredness of the Bible (see GENDER). Central to the story will be the feelings of Dinah's brothers about what has happened, while the feelings of Dinah—the person to whom it has happened—are nowhere expressed.

Dinah's brothers are "very wroth," feeling that this Hivite prince has "wrought folly in Israel in lying with Jacob's daughter, which thing ought not to be done." It must be a pretty tense meeting when Shechem and his father Hamor (whose name means "ass" in Hebrew) come to see Jacob and his sons. Hamor speaks to them not of one marriage but several, that the Hebrews may "dwell and trade" prosperously with the Canaanites. "Make ye marriages with us," says Hamor, "and give your daughters unto us, and take our daughters unto you." Shechem then offers Jacob's sons whatever they want for the right to wed Dinah.

Jacob's sons answer "deceitfully." They first say that they cannot give their sister "to one that is uncircumcised," as that would be "a reproach" to the Hebrew people. (See CIRCUMCISION: "SIGN OF THE COVENANT.") But they then say they'll agree to the marriages proposed if "every male of you be circumcised." Then, say the Hebrews, "we will become one people." If there is no such circumcision, "then will we take our daughter," they warn, and "be gone."

Hamor and Shechem go straight home to urge circumcision upon the men of their city (named Shechem). The two preach prosperity should the Hebrews dwell among them: "Shall not their cattle and their substance and every beast of theirs be ours?" To the men of Shechem, this sounds like a fair trade for their foreskins, which they proceed to have cut off.

Three days later, with these fellows all lying around sore, Jacob's sons come and put them out of their misery. The two tribes of Simeon and Levi (Dinah's full brothers) are the first to fall upon the city. They kill Hamor and Shechem and all the other males in town. The tribes of the other sons follow, looting the city and taking all its new widows captive. They fetch Dinah from the house of Shechem.

Jacob complains to Simeon and Levi that what they have done will make him "stink among the inhabitants of the land," who far outnumber the Hebrews. "I shall be destroyed," frets Jacob, "I and my house."

The sons reply only with a bitter question: "Should (Shechem) deal with our sister as with a harlot?"   (GENESIS 34)

⇒ JUDAH AND TAMAR

SHEM, FIRST OF THE SEMITES

Noah's firstborn son, and nominally the world's first Semite, was ninety-eight years old when he went aboard his six-hundred-year-old father's ark to survive the Flood. According to extrabiblical tradition, Noah forbade any sex between his three sons and their wives during their long stay on the ark. (Also forbidden, says this tradition, was sex between the animals.) There was plenty of time for sex later, as after the Flood Shem (Hebrew "renown") not only fathered a son named Arphaxad but "begat sons and daughters" for five hundred more years.

The line from Shem to Terah (father of Abraham)—including Eber, hence the term "Hebrew"—is listed in Genesis 11 as "the generations of Shem," eight individuals who "begat sons and daughters" while living an average of three hundred and twenty-five years. Thus Shem helped his brothers Ham and Japheth repopulate the earth: "Of them was the whole earth overspread."   (GEN. 7:13, 9:18-19; 11:10-32)

⇒ ABRAHAM AND SARAH

SODOM(Y) AND GOMORRAH

In the days of the patriarch Abraham, there is a great outcry against the sinfulness of Sodom and Gomorrah, two Canaanite cities of the Jordan plain. The Hebrew God Yahweh sends two angels to Sodom to see if things there are as bad as he's heard. (He tells Abraham, whose nephew Lot lives in Sodom, that he will spare the city if the angels find as few as ten righteous men there.)

It is night when the angels reach Sodom. They run into Lot, who, not even aware they are angels, graciously puts them up for the night. It is not bedtime, though, before the men of Sodom—every one of them, young and old—surround Lot's house. They ask Lot where "the men" are who are staying with him. "Bring them out," say the Sodomites, "that we may know them."

Lot knows what they mean, and is required by the code of hospitality to protect his two guests. He goes outside to talk to the mob. (His guests, being angels, are capable of protecting themselves, but Lot wouldn't know an angel if he saw one.)

"I have two daughters," Lot tells the mob, "which have not known man." He offers to bring out both maidens for their pleasure: "do ye to them as is good in your eyes: only unto these men do nothing." But the mob says "Stand back," and is about to break in when the angels intervene. Pulling Lot into the house, the angels shut the door, then strike the Sodomites with blindness, leaving them groping in vain for the door.

The angels tell Lot to get all his family and flee Sodom, for "the Lord hath sent us to destroy it." Having other daughters who are married, Lot goes to his sons-in-law, but they just laugh at his story. In the morning the angels escort Lot, his wife, and two virgin daughters out of the city, then "brimstone and fire" rain down "from the Lord out of heaven" upon Sodom and Gomorrah. Told not to look back, Lot's wife does so—no doubt thinking, as notes Rebecca Goldstein, of her poor married daughters—and is turned into a pillar of salt.

It is from Sodom, of course, that we get the word sodomy. According to Raphael Patai (writing in 1959), homosexuality was "rampant" in the ancient Near East, with the mob at Sodom, like the one later at Gibeah (see BENJAMIN: "A RAVENOUS WOLF"), "addicted to homosexual practices." Robert Goss offers an alternative explanation for the mob's behavior: anal penetration was an ancient way of asserting domination over "strangers, the conquered, and trespassers." (According to Jewish legend, there was even a law in Sodom that all strangers were to be so penetrated [Ginzberg 1:254].)

Whatever the mob's motive, there is a consensus among scholars that the basic sin of the Sodomites on the night in question is their violation of the code of hospitality, a code of vital importance among ancient Near Eastern nomads. But what are we to make of Lot offering his two virgin daughters in the name of protecting his guests? Though the Genesis narrative passes no judgment, Lot's attempt to avoid violence against men by substituting violence against women—in this case his own flesh and blood—has no scriptural justification (see Sharon Place Jeansonne). The offer speaks volumes, however, about the male-centered nature of biblical times. (See GENDER.)

(GEN. 18:20-19:26)   ⇒ LOT AND HIS DAUGHTERS

SOLOMON AND HIS "OUTLANDISH WOMEN"

King Solomon of Israel believed in conspicuous consumption. At his table, for example, were consumed one hundred sheep and thirty oxen a day, not counting all the venison and fowl. But then everyone in Israel was "eating and drinking, and making merry." There was "peace on all sides," and every man dwelt safely "under his vine and under his fig tree, from Dan even to Beersheba." Surely a king ruling over such idyllic times had a right to his excess.

Solomon was also a conspicous lover. He "loved many strange women," meaning foreign ones. He loved home-grown ones too, for a total of at least one thousand—"he had seven hundred wives, princesses, and three hundred concubines." The sheer number may have emboldened his half-brother Adonijah to ask for one of the royal concubines—Abishag the Shunammite—in marriage. Solomon, viewing the request as a sign of treacherous ambition, had his half-brother executed.

When Solomon wasn't eating or making love, he was apparently composing: renowned for his wisdom, "he spake three thousand proverbs, and his songs were a thousand and five." He did find time to hold court, hence his judgment in the case of two harlots, each claiming to be the same child's mother. When Solomon ordered that the child be literally divided between them, the harlot who was lying agreed, while the real mother, to save the child's life, relinquished her claim to the infant. The wise Solomon then gave the real mother her child. (One wonders if Solomon, with all those wives and concubines, could judge who was the mother of whom among his own children.)

And then there's the Queen of Sheba. Hearing of Solomon's wisdom, if not of his sexual stamina, this queen came from Sheba (in Arabia or perhaps Ethiopia) "with a very great train" to Jerusalem, "to prove him with hard questions." When Solomon had answered each one, and shown her all the splendors of his court, the queen was left breathless. "It was a true report that I heard," she said, but "the half was not told me." (She later adds, "Happy are thy wives," the KJV mistranslating the last word as "men."). Before she went home, we are told that "king Solomon gave the queen of Sheba all her desire." Whether that included sexual desire is not stated (aside from the double entendres), but according to extrabiblical tradition it did.

But women, alas, brought Solomon into divine disfavor, despite the fact that he built the first temple, "the house of the Lord," in Jerusalem. For all his "outlandish" (that is, foreign) women (as Nehemiah [13:26] later calls them) had their own foreign deities. This led Solomon into idolatry, as he catered to "all his strange wives, which burnt incense and sacrificed unto their gods." Thus the Lord "was angry with Solomon," and determined as punishment to divide the kingdom following Solomon's reign. (It would not be divided in Solomon's days, Yahweh told him, "for David thy father's sake.") The political stage for division was already set, in the form of growing popular discontent: the king's high living and building projects meant higher taxes and forced labor for those who had earlier made merry under fig tree and vine.

Upon his death, Solomon was succeeded by his son Rehoboam as king of Israel. But as Yahweh ordained, the kingdom then divided in two (Israel and Judah), as all of Israel's tribes except Judah chose Jeroboam, the son of one of

Solomon's servants, as king. Because of Solomon's excesses, after his day "there was none that followed the house of David, but the tribe of Judah only."

(1 KINGS 4:1-34; 10:1-13; 11:1-13,42-43; 12:1-20)

⇒ MAACHAH AND REHOBOAM

SONG OF SOLOMON

"Let him kiss me with the kisses of his mouth: for (his) love is better than wine." So begins "the song of songs" (*shir hashirim*), not really a song but an erotic love poem—or rather an amalgam of erotic love poems—that somehow found its way into the Hebrew Bible. And it's a good thing it did, opined Christian theologian Dietrich Bonhoeffer, considering "all those who believe that the restraint of passion is Christian."

There is little restraint in *shir hashirim*, in which two unnamed lovers long for each other ("His left hand should be under my head, and his right hand should embrace me" [8:3]), admire each other anatomically ("Thy navel is like a round goblet, which wanteth not liquor" [7:2]), and meet for lovemaking ("He shall lie down all night betwixt my breasts" [1:13]), in village, vineyard, and field (7:11-12) ("our bed is green" [1:16]).

Metaphorical gardens, spices, and fruit are prominent in the Song's lovemaking imagery. The woman compares her "beloved" (*dodi*) to an apple tree: "I sat down under his shadow with great delight, and his fruit was sweet to my taste" (2:3). Her *dodi*, not to be outdone, likens her to a palm tree: "I will take hold of the boughs thereof," and "thy breasts shall be as clusters of the vine" (7:8). Her lover describes the woman as "a garden enclosed," with "a fountain sealed" (4:12), and her meaning is clear when the woman says that her beloved "has gone down into his garden, to the beds of spices, to feed in the gardens, and to gather lilies" (6:2). ("My beloved is mine," she says earlier, "and I am his: he feedeth among the lilies" [2:16].)

The book's title in the KJV is the Song of Solomon, but there is little scholarly support for the notion that this is a work of the Israelite king. (It is also known as the Song of Songs, and in the Catholic Bible as Canticles.) Given the prominence of the woman in the lovers' dialogue, the Song could well be the work of a woman. It is uncertain whether her statement "I am dark, but comely" (NRSV "black and beautiful") (1:5) means she is of African descent, as Bellis and others suggest, or (as the next verse implies) dark from having to work in the sun (1:6). Renita J. Weems points out that in any case the woman, being presented in the first person rather than through a narrator, is "the only unmediated female voice in scripture." The work is also exceptional for its celebration of physical love without reference to procreation, and for its egalitarian nature. In the relationship between the two lovers, "there is no male dominance," in Phyllis Trible's words, "no female subordination, and no stereotyping of either sex." (See GENDER: "MALE AND FEMALE CREATED HE THEM.") However, the patriarchal subordination of women again rears its head when "the watchmen" who patrol the city find the woman out looking for her lover: "they smote me," she tells us, "they wounded me" (5:7).

Some of the cooings of the Song's ancient Near Eastern lovers may now seem rather quaint. It is questionable whether a woman today would be flattered to hear she has hair like "a flock of goats" (4:1), or that her nose is like "the tower of Lebanon which looketh toward Damascus" (7:4). Still, the passion that is expressed in the Song is timeless: "Set me as a seal upon thine heart, as a seal upon thine arm: for love is strong as death; jealousy is cruel as the grave" (8:6). Efforts to interpret it all as an allegory of Yahweh's love for Israel, or Christ's love for the church, are unconvincing in light of the Song's straightforward eroticism. It's a bit much to have Christ telling the church that "the joints of thy thighs are like jewels" (7:1), or to accept the view of Hippolytus (cited in William E. Phipps's *Genesis and Gender*) that the man's praise of his lover's breasts—"Thy two breasts are like two young roes that are twins" (7:3)—means that the Old and New Testaments are glorious.

SONG OF SONGS: "Among the Lilies"

See SONG OF SOLOMON.

SONS OF GOD: "They Took Them Wives"

Male members of God's heavenly court are mentioned three times in the book of Job: called *bene ha Elohim* ("sons of God"), they twice present themselves (Satan among them) before God (1:6, 2:1), and are described as shouting for joy at the creation (38:7). (Similarly, heavenly beings are referred to as *bene elim* ["sons of gods"] in Ps. 29:1, and *bene Elyon* ["sons of the Most High"] in Ps. 89:6.) According to the book of Genesis (6:1-4), some of these divine beings also enjoyed themselves by mating with earthly women: "the sons of God" saw that "the daughters of men . . . were fair, and they took them wives of all which they chose." The sons of God then "came in unto" these earthly wives, and "they bare children to them." The children were giants called the Nephilim, "the mighty men that were of old, men of renown."

Though originally, it appears, a tradition to account for the presence of "giants in the earth in those days" (Gen. 6:4), the story of the sons of God and the daughters of men is used in Genesis to help illustrate the earthly wickedness—these were apparently bad giants—that led God to send Noah's Flood. Thus the Nephilim passage is followed by the statement that "God saw that the wickedness of man was great in the earth," man's every thought being "only evil continually" (Gen. 6:5).

In the pseudepigraphical 1 Enoch (6-14), the sons of God are called the Watchers, angels who take earthly women for themselves and father giants who plague mankind. God has the fallen angels bound inside the earth till the day of judgment. (See also Jubilees 5:1-10.) In the New Testament, 2 Peter 2:4 tells how these angels were cast "down to hell, . . . to be reserved unto judgment," and Jude 6 refers to the angels who "kept not their first estate" and are "in everlasting chains" till judgment day. It would also seem to be Genesis's lustful sons of God to whom Paul refers in 1 Cor. 11:10: praying or prophesying women should have their heads covered, says the Apostle, "because of the angels." ⇒ NOAH

SUSANNA AND THE ELDERS

In Babylon during the exile (sixth century B.C.E.), his fellow Jews are very fond of visiting the home of Joakim. For Joakim is rich, a fine garden adjoins his house, and he has a beautiful wife named Susanna ("lily"). Two Jewish elders, who as judges hold court at Joakim's place, enjoy watching Susanna stroll in her husband's garden every day after the other folks leave at noon. Each elder is too ashamed to tell the other, however, of the lust Susanna stirs in his heart.

One day the two elders leave Joakim's at mealtime, parting outside the house. No sooner do they part than each one doubles back, wanting to see more of Susanna. Running into each other, the elders mutually confess their overpowering desire for this woman. They now watch and wait for the day when together they can catch her alone.

One day Susanna, watched by the two hiding elders, enters the garden with two maids. It is hot and Susanna wants to bathe. The two maids, following Susanna's orders, shut the garden doors and leave by side doors to go fetch ointments for her bath.

As soon as the maids are gone, the two elders run over to the surprised Susanna. "The garden doors are shut, no one sees us," they tell her, "and we are in love with you," so "lie with us." If she refuses, she is told, they will testify that a young man was with her and that is why she sent away the maids.

They have Susanna in a bind. To refuse means she will then be falsely accused, and to consent would be her death (the penalty for adultery). She chooses to refuse rather than to sin before God. She cries out, the elders shout against her, and as household servants come running to see what is wrong, the elders make their false accusation.

The next day Susanna is brought before an assembly in Joakim's house. The two elders testify that they were walking in the garden when they saw her enter with her maids, send the maids away, and then lie with a young man who came out of hiding. They claim that they ran over and grabbed the man, but he was too strong to hold and got away. They then seized Susanna, who refused to tell them who the young man was.

The assembly believes these two elders—they're judges of the people, after all—and condemns Susanna to die for adultery. Crying out, she protests her innocence in a prayer to God. As she is being led away, suddenly a loud voice is heard: "I am innocent of this woman's blood."

All eyes turn to Daniel, a young man who has been moved by God, in response to Susanna's prayer, to step forward. He berates the adjourning assembly for condemning to death a daughter of Israel without determining the facts. Reassemble, he tells them, for these two elders have borne false witness.

Reconvening, the assembly allows Daniel to question the two elders separately, each out of the other's hearing. "You relic of wicked days," Daniel addresses the first one, "under which tree did you see them making love?"

"Under a mastic tree," says the elder.

The angel of God, Daniel tells him, will now "cut you in two" ("cut" being a pun on "mastic" in the original Greek) for lying.

The second elder is brought in. "You offspring of Canaan and not Judah," Daniel addresses him, "under which tree did you catch them making love?"

"Under an evergreen oak," says the elder.

"You also have lied," Daniel tells him, and by the angel of God will be "split in two" (a pun on evergreen oak).

The assembly praises God, and puts the two elders to death for bearing false witness. Joakim and the rest of her kin thank God that Susanna is innocent, and Daniel is a young man who will be heard from again. (See the book of Daniel and the apocryphal Bel and the Dragon.) (APOCRYPHA: SUSANNA) ⇒ ESTHER

T

TAMAR AND AMNON

See AMNON AND TAMAR.

TAMAR AND JUDAH

See JUDAH AND TAMAR.

TOBIAS AND SARAH

See SARAH AND TOBIAS.

TRANSVESTISM: "Abominable to the Lord"

"A woman shall not wear a man's clothing," says the book of Deuteronomy (22:5), "nor shall a man put on a woman's garment." This outlawing of transvestism or cross-dressing is one of several commandments against the mixing of created kinds of things (Lev. 19:19; Deut. 22:9-11), a mingling considered contrary to God's order of creation. A farmer, for example, could not plow with an ox and an ass together, and no one could wear a garment in which were mingled wool and linen. Similarly, cross-dressing was a disorder—a mental one, some would argue—or mixing of kinds.

No penalty for transvestism is prescribed, but those who transgress—or cross-dress—are called "abominable to the Lord your God" (Deut. 22:5).

U-V

URIAH THE HITTITE

See BATHSHEBA: "I AM WITH CHILD."

VASHTI, QUEEN OF PERSIA

See ESTHER: "THE MAIDEN WHO PLEASES THE KING."

VIRGIN BIRTH: "Child of the Holy Ghost"

In Palestine during the reign of Caesar Augustus, a virgin named Mary, espoused to Joseph of the house of David, is visited by the angel Gabriel. "Behold, thou shalt conceive in thy womb, and bring forth a son," Gabriel tells Mary, "and shalt call his name Jesus." The angel then describes the son's destined greatness, but Mary is puzzled about the conception: "How shall this be," she asks, "seeing I know not a man?"

"The Holy Ghost shall come upon thee," explains Gabriel, "and the power of the Highest shall overshadow thee: therefore also that holy thing which shall be born of thee shall be called the Son of God."

Sure enough, Mary is soon "found to be with child of the Holy Ghost." Joseph has some doubts, though, about the paternity, and is about to divorce her, till things are divinely explained in a dream. Joseph doesn't "know" Mary until she has borne her son Jesus. According to Catholic belief, Joseph doesn't even know her after that. Immaculately conceived by Saint Anne (see the noncanonical book of James), Mary remains forever a virgin, Joseph's other children considered to be from some previous marriage.

The cult of Mary the perpetual Virgin reflects the rise in Christianity of an ascetic attitude, not found in biblical Hebrew religion, toward sexuality. The virgin birth of Christ is found only in the gospels of Matthew and Luke. It is mentioned nowhere else in the New Testament. And by denying Joseph a role in Christ's conception, the virgin birth contradicts Matthew's own contention, through a lengthy opening genealogy, that Jesus was "the son of David, the son of Abraham," by direct descent. The Apostle Paul (writing years before the gospels were written) also posits a Davidic human father of Christ in Rom. 1:3-4, stating that Jesus "was made of the seed of David according to the flesh," and "was *declared* to be the Son of God" (emphasis added) by virtue of the resurrection. It is strange indeed, if belief in the virgin birth of Christ was current among Christians of Paul's day, that Paul is silent on that belief even when discussing how Christ was "made" and became God's Son.

Matthew seems determined, though, to contradict himself, by appealing to the prophet Isaiah. But Matthew's effort to find a virginal conception foretold in the Old Testament—"Behold, a virgin shall be with child" (Matt. 1.23, based on Isa. 7:14)— takes some liberty with the original text. Isaiah's sign of Immanuel (7:14), which is non-Messianic, is a "young woman" (Hebrew *almah*) who conceives. The Hebrew word for virgin is *betulah*, not *almah*. Yet *almah* was translated into Greek as *parthenos*, "virgin," which Matthew, working from a Greek text, found much to his liking.

A miraculous birth story about an important personage was nothing new in the ancient world. Plato and Alexander, among others, were said to be sons of deities by mortal women. Interestingly, the second-century writer Celsus claimed that Jesus was actually the illegitimate son of a Roman centurion named

Panthera. (For what it's worth, the tombstone of a first-century centurion named Panthera of Sidon has been found in Germany. See Ian Wilson's *Jesus: The Evidence.*)

In sum, the importance of Jesus' virginal conception as an article of Christian faith is debatable. (See Jane Schaberg.) It was declared one of Christianity's "five fundamentals"—hence the term fundamentalism—by a conservative Bible conference in 1895. But it can also be argued that Jesus was divinely adopted—as Paul puts it in Rom. 1:4, "declared to be the Son of God." At Jesus' baptism, "the Holy Ghost descended" in the form of a dove, and a voice from heaven said, "Thou art my beloved Son" (Luke 3:21-22), with some of the ancient source texts adding, "Today I have begotten thee."

(MATT. 1:18-25; LUKE 1:26-38, 2:1-7)
⇒ HEROD AND THE DANCE OF SALOME

VIRGINITY: "The Bridegroom Rejoiceth"

In the patriarchal society of the Hebrews, a maiden was under the control of her father till she married, at which time control passed to her husband. Till married she was to remain a virgin (*betulah*), for which "the bridegroom rejoiceth" (Isa. 62:5); to have premarital sex with a man was "to play the whore in her father's house," and was punishable by death (Deut. 22:13-21). This tight control over women's sexuality was grounded in economics, not ethics. Female virginity until marriage helped insure knowledge of who was the father of whom, knowledge essential in a patrilineal system (one in which descent and inheritance are reckoned through the male line). Consequently a virgin of marriageable age had economic value, through the bride price or *mohar* payable to her father (see MARRIAGE). A non-virgin, bringing a lower bride price if any, was at best damaged goods. (See Archer's *Her Price Is Beyond Rubies.*)

A girl's non-virginity might not be suspected, of course, when a marriage was arranged. According to the law, unless her parents could produce "the tokens of the damsel's virginity" (i.e., a bloody sheet from the marriage bed), a new bride accused by her husband of having not been found a virgin was to be stoned to death by "the men of her city" (Deut. 22:13-21)—a double standard and then some, there being no requirement that the accuser be a virgin himself.

There were penalties, though, for a single man having sex with a virgin. It was the same as adultery (for which the penalty was death) if the virgin was betrothed to another man (Deut. 22:22-27); if she was not betrothed, the man had to pay a bride price and marry her (Deut. 22:28-29).

There are two noteworthy competitions involving virgins in the Bible. When the aged King David needs someone to warm him in bed, a search "throughout all the coasts of Israel" for a suitable virgin produces Abishag the Shunammite—though even she can't seem to warm him enough ("the king knew her not") (1 Kgs. 1:1-4). In the book of Esther, when King Ahasuerus of Persia needs a new queen, virgins from throughout the realm are brought to Ahasuerus for tryouts, with Esther winning the crown.

Hebrew priests were to marry only virgins (Lev. 21:13), though Ezekiel (44:22) allows them to marry also widows of priests. Hebrew warriors could keep captured virgins as war booty, either enslaving or (as mandated in Deuteronomy) marrying them (Num. 31:17-18,35; Deut. 21:10-14; Judg. 21:8-14). At times the Hebrews themselves are metaphorically depicted as a victimized virgin (Jer. 14:17; Lam. 1:15, 2:13; Amos 5:2).

Since Hebrew men and women were expected to get married and have children, and since the enjoyment of sex was encouraged within the confines of marriage (Deut. 24:5; Prov. 5:18-19), the idea of lifelong virginity as a virtue was foreign to the biblical Hebrews. This may be seen in the story of Jephthah's daughter. When the judge Jephthah, to keep an ill-advised vow, must execute his young virgin daughter, she is first given two months to "bewail (her) virginity," that is, to mourn the fact that she must die a childless woman (Judg. 11:30-40).

Radically different is the Christian view found in Rev. 14:4, in which 144,000 males, "redeemed from the earth" and in the company of Christ the Lamb, are praised for being virgins, "they which were not defiled by women." Such antisexual sentiments (and hence the glorification of virginity) in the New Testament reflect the influence of ascetic and misogynistic thought in the Greco-Roman world, as well as the early Christian view that the world is about to end and that virgins and everyone else should therefore remain as they are. In 2 Cor. 11:2, the Apostle Paul refers to the church itself as "a chaste virgin" presented by Paul to Christ. (See also GENDER; LOVEMAKING; PAUL; and VIRGIN BIRTH.)

W

WHOREDOM: "Under Every Green Tree"

See HARLOTRY: "A-WHORING AFTER OTHER GODS" *and* PROSTITUTION: IS NOTHING SACRED?

WISDOM: She's a Lady

See YAHWEH: "THY MAKER IS THINE HUSBAND."

WOMEN: "In Silence with All Subjection"

See GENDER: "MALE AND FEMALE CREATED HE THEM"; LOVEMAKING: TO KNOW IN THE BIBLICAL SENSE; MARRIAGE: "THEY SHALL BE ONE FLESH"; *and* PAUL: "BETTER TO MARRY THAN TO BURN."

Y

YAHWEH: "Thy Maker is Thine Husband"

The Hebrew God Yahweh is conceived of biblically as a male deity, with the covenant relationship between him and Israel often portrayed as that of a marriage between husband and wife. (The other name by which the deity is most often referred to in the Hebrew Bible is *Elohim* [translated "God"], an originally plural form meaning "gods." "The LORD" in English versions translates Yahweh —the assumed pronunciation of YHWH [a name of uncertain meaning], there being no vowels in the original Hebrew text.)

The perception of God as masculine is of course not surprising in a patriarchal or male-ruled society. As noted by Susan Ackerman, there are some feminizations of Yahweh in Isaiah (e.g., "As one whom his mother comforteth, so will I comfort you" [66:13]; see also 42:14 and 49:15). But then Isaiah also refers to kings as "nursing fathers" (49:23) and to daughters who "shalt suck the breasts of kings" (60:16), words that cannot be taken literally. In any case, Yahweh outside of some Isaianic imagery is masculine in the Hebrew Bible.

In the New Testament, "God" translates the Greek *Theos*, with God remaining a male deity. Thus Jesus regularly uses the word Father (Greek *Pater*, in Jesus' Aramaic *Abba*) for God (e.g., Matt. 6:8-9; Mark 14:36; Luke 10:21; John 17:1; see also Paul's use in Rom. 8:15 and Gal. 4:6). Elaine Pagels points out that some Christian Gnostics thought of the divine in both masculine and feminine terms, with Jesus referring to the Holy

Spirit as his Mother in the Gospel of Thomas and in the Gospel to the Hebrews, and with the Apocryphon of John describing the Trinity as Father, Mother, and Son. As Pagels notes, however, such views were suppressed as heretical, with none of the Gnostic texts included in the New Testament canon. (See Robinson's *The Nag Hammadi Library.*)

There is archeological evidence that at least some ancient Hebrews perceived of Yahweh as having a consort or female companion (see ASHERAH: THE LORD GOD'S LADY?). This could be the origin of the mysterious Lady Wisdom found in Proverbs and the Apocrypha. (She is in some of the Gnostic texts as well.) Wisdom (Hebrew *hokma*, a feminine noun) is personified in Proverbs not only as a woman but as a preexistent entity with Yahweh. "The Lord possessed me in the beginning of his way," says Lady Wisdom, "before his works of old, . . . and I was daily his delight, rejoicing always before him" (Prov. 8:22,30). It was through Wisdom that Yahweh "founded the earth" (3:19), she is "a tree of life" to those who lay hold of her (3:18), and she offers to reward all who seek her: "I love them that love me; and those that seek me early shall find me" (8:17).

In the Apocrypha, Lady Wisdom is identified with the Torah or biblical law (Sirach 24:23; Baruch 4:1). In the New Testament, the preexistent Word (Greek *Logos*) at the beginning of the Gospel of John is reminiscent of Wisdom, and in 1 Cor. 1:24 Paul calls Christ "the wisdom of God" (Greek *Theou Sophia*).

The metaphor of Yahweh and the Hebrew people as husband and wife is found first in the book of Hosea, and continues in the books of Isaiah, Jeremiah, and Ezekiel. It is a troubled marriage, for despite Yahweh's "love toward the children of Israel," they "look to other gods" (Hos. 3:1). The wife's infidelity is thus a metaphor for the Israelite people's idolatry. (See HARLOTRY: "A-WHORING AFTER OTHER GODS.") "Thy maker is thine husband," Isaiah tells Israel, yet she beds down with others (Isa. 54:5; 57:7-8). "Turn, O backsliding children," Yahweh pleads in Jeremiah (3:14), "for I am married unto you." At one point Yahweh divorces Israel for her adultery, only to have "her treacherous sister Judah" commit adultery also (Jer.

3:8). Ezekiel 23 allegorizes Samaria and Jerusalem, the Israelite and Judahite capitals, as two sisters with a host of foreign lovers while both are married to Yahweh.

Particularly disturbing to feminist commentators are the biblical passages that describe Yahweh's brutal punishment of the women who symbolize Israel's unfaithfulness. As noted by Kathleen M. O'Connor, the portrayal of physical abuse by the divine in such passages implicitly condones such behavior in humans. Just as Yahweh rapes Babylon in Isa. 47:1-4, so he helps the Babylonians rape Jerusalem in Jer. 13:26 (see RAPE.) In Lamentations, Yahweh trods "the virgin" Jerusalem "as in a winepress" (1:15), and in Ezekiel he tells his wife Oholibah (Jerusalem), "I will raise up thy lovers against thee," and they will "strip thee out of thy clothes"; they will take away not only "thy sons and thy daughters" but "thy nose and thine ears," and "thus will I make thy lewdness to cease from thee" (23:22-27).

Needless to say, the thought behind these metaphors of Yahweh the husband physically abusing his wife presents a challenge to modern biblical interpreters. Through such imagery "the Bible," writes Sharon H. Ringe in *The Women's Bible Commentary*, "seems to bless the harm and abuse with which women live and sometimes die." The brutality seems hardly ameliorated by Yahweh's assurances to his mutilated wife of a brighter tomorrow, for they make God sound like the stereotypical wife beater who minimizes what he has done and promises not to do it again: "In a little wrath I hid my face from thee for a moment; but with everlasting kindness will I have mercy on thee. . . . . Again I will build thee, and thou shalt be built, O virgin of Israel, . . . and shalt go forth in the dances of them that make merry" (Isa. 54:8; Jer. 31:4).

Z

ZANAH/ZONAH

See HARLOTRY: "A-WHORING AFTER OTHER GODS" *and* PROSTITUTION: IS NOTHING SACRED?

ZECHARIAH AND ELIZABETH

See ELIZABETH AND ZECHARIAH.

ZILPAH THE HANDMAID

See JACOB AND LABAN'S DAUGHTERS.

ZIMRI: Too Cozy with Cozbi

See COZBI AND ZIMRI.

ZIPPORAH AND MOSES

See MOSES AND ZIPPORAH.

Bibliography

Achtemeier, Paul J., ed. *Harper's Bible Dictionary*. San Francisco: Harper & Row, 1985.

Ackerman, Susan. " 'And the Women Knead Dough': The Worship of the Queen of Heaven in Sixth-Century Judah." In Day, pp. 109-124.

_____. "Isaiah." In Newsom and Ringe, pp. 161-168.

Alpert, Rebecca. "Finding Our Past: A Lesbian Interpretation of the Book of Ruth." In Kates and Reimer, pp. 91-96.

Archer, Léonie J. *Her Price Is Beyond Rubies: The Jewish Woman in Graeco-Roman Palestine*. Sheffield, England: Sheffield Academic Press, 1990.

Barnstone, Willis, ed. *The Other Bible*. San Francisco: Harper & Row, 1984.

Barr, James. *The Garden of Eden and the Hope of Immortality*. Minneapolis: Fortress Press, 1992.

Bellis, Alice Ogden. *Helpmates, Harlots, and Heroes: Women's Stories in the Hebrew Bible*. Louisville: Westminster/John Knox, 1994.

Bird, Phyllis A. "Prostitution." In Metzger and Coogan, pp. 623-624.

_____. " 'To Play the Harlot': An Inquiry into an Old Testament Metaphor." In Day, pp. 75-94.

Black, Matthew, and Rowley, H. H., eds. *Peake's Commentary on the Bible*. Nashville: Thomas Nelson Pubers, 1962.

Bonhoeffer, Dietrich. *Letters and Papers from Prison*. New York: Macmillan, 1972.

Boswell, John. *Christianity, Social Tolerance, and Homosexuality*. Chicago: University of Chicago Press, 1980.

Brockington, L. H. "I and II Samuel." In Black and Rowley, pp. 318-337.

Buchmann, Christina, and Spiegel, Celina, ed. *Out of the Garden: Women Writers on the Bible*. New York: Fawcett Columbine, 1994.

Burchard, C., tr. "Joseph and Aseneth." In Charlesworth, pp. 177-247.

Calloway, Mary Chilton. "Women in the Old Testament." In Smith and Hoffmann, pp. 197-211.

Charlesworth, James H., ed. *The Old Testament Pseudepigrapha*. Garden City, NY: Doubleday, 1985.

Cole, William Graham. *Sex and Love in the Bible*. New York: Association Press, 1959.

Comstock, Gary David. *Gay Theology without Apology*. Cleveland, Ohio: Pilgrim Press, 1993.

Countryman, L. William. *Dirt, Greed, and Sex: Sexual Ethics in the New Testament and Their Implications for Today*. Philadelphia: Fortress Press, 1988.

Darr, Katheryn Pfisterer. "Ezekiel." In Newsom and Ringe, pp. 183-190.

Davies, G. Henton. "Deuteronomy." In Black and Rowley, pp. 269-284.

Day, Peggy L., ed. *Gender and Difference in Ancient Israel*. Minneapolis: Fortress Press, 1989.

Dever, William G. *Recent Archaeological Discoveries and Biblical Research*. Seattle: University of Washington Press, 1990.

Donfried, Karl Paul. "Love." In Achtemeier, pp. 578-581.

Douglas, Mary. *Purity and Danger: An Analysis of Concepts of Pollution and Taboo*. London: Routledge & Kegan Paul, 1966.

Eisenman, Robert, and Wise, Michael. *The Dead Sea Scrolls Uncovered: The First Complete Translation of 50 Key Documents Withheld for Over 35 Years*. New York: Penguin, 1993.

Fiorenza, Elisabeth Schüssler. *In Memory of Her: A Feminist Theological Reconstruction of Christian Origins*. New

York: Crossroad, 1983.

Fiorenza, Elisabeth Schüssler. "Interpreting Patriarchal Traditions." In Russell 1976, pp. 39-61.

Frazer, Sir James. *The New Golden Bough*, edited by Theodor H. Gaster. New York: New American Library, 1964.

Freeman, David Noel, ed. *The Anchor Bible Dictionary.* New York: Doubleday, 1992.

Frymer-Kensky, Tikva. "Deuteronomy." In Newsom and Ringe, pp. 52-62.

_____. "Harlot." In Achtemeier, p. 374.

_____. *In the Wake of the Goddesses: Women, Culture, and the Biblical Transformation of Pagan Myth.* New York: Fawcett Columbine, 1992.

_____. "Sex and Sexuality." In Freeman, v. 5, pp. 1144-1146.

Funk, Robert W., Hoover, Roy W., and the Jesus Seminar. *The Five Gospels: The Search for the Authentic Words of Jesus.* New York: Macmillan, 1993.

Furnish, Victor Paul. "Homosexuality." In Achtemeier, p. 402.

Gammie, John G. "Loving-kindness." In Achtemeier, p. 581.

Gaster, Theodor H. *Myth, Legend, and Custom in the Old Testament.* New York: Harper & Row, 1969.

Ghougassian, Joseph P. *Toward Women: A Study of the Origins of Western Attitudes Through Greco-Roman Philosophy.* San Diego: Lukas & Sons, 1977.

Ginzberg, Louis. *The Legends of the Jews.* Philadelphia: Jewish Publications Society of America, 1909.

Goldstein, Rebecca. "Looking Back at Lot's Wife." In Buchmann and Spiegel, pp. 3-12.

Goodfriend, Elaine Adler. "Prostitution (OT)." In Freeman v. 5, pp. 505-510.

Goss, Robert. *Jesus Acted Up: A Gay and Lesbian Manifesto.* San Francisco: HarperSanFrancisco, 1993.

Gottwald, Norman K. "Deuteronomy." In Laymon, pp. 100-121.

Graves, Robert, and Patai, Raphael. *Hebrew Myths: The Book of Genesis.* New York: McGraw-Hill, 1966.

Hackett, Jo Ann. "1 and 2 Samuel." In Newsom and Ringe, pp.

85-95.

Haskins, Susan. *Mary Magdalen: Myth and Metaphor*. New York: Harcourt, Brace & Co., 1993.

Hiers, Richard H. "Transfer of Property by Inheritance and Bequest in Biblical Law and Tradition." *The Journal of Law and Religion* 10, no. 1 (1993-94), 121-155.

Hooke, Samuel H. "Genesis." In Black and Rowley, pp. 175-207.

Horner, Tom. *Sex in the Bible*. Rutland, VT: Tuttle, 1974.

Hurley, James B. *Man and Woman in Biblical Perspective*. Grand Rapids, MI: Academie Books, 1981.

Isenberg, Wesley, tr. "The Gospel of Philip (II, 3)." In Robinson, pp. 139-160.

Jeansonne, Sharon Pace. *The Women of Genesis: From Sarah to Potiphar's Wife*. Minneapolis: Fortress Press, 1990.

Kates, Judith A., and Reimer, Gail Twersky, ed. *Reading Ruth: Contemporary Women Reclaim a Sacred Story*. New York: Ballantine, 1994.

Kee, H. C., tr. "Testaments of the Twelve Patriarchs." In Charlesworth v. 1, pp. 775-828.

LaCocque, André. *The Feminine Unconventional: Four Subversive Figures in Israel's Tradition*. Minneapolis: Fortress Press, 1990.

Larue, Gerald. *Sex and the Bible*. Buffalo, NY: Prometheus Books, 1983.

Laymon, Charles M., ed. *The Interpreter's One-Volume Commentary on the Bible*. Nashville: Abingdon Press, 1971.

Lemaire, André. "Who or What was Yahweh's Asherah?" *Biblical Archaeology Review* 10, no. 6 (November/December 1984), 42-51.

Lerner, Gerda. *The Creation of Patriarchy*. New York: Oxford University Press, 1986.

Levine, Amy-Jill. "Ruth." In Newsome and Ringe, pp. 78-84.

Mauchline, John. "I and II Kings." In Black and Rowley, pp. 338-356.

McAfee, Gene. "Sex." In Metzger and Coogan, pp. 690-692.

McKenzie, Steven L. "Ham/Canaan, Cursing of." In Metzger

and Coogan, p. 268.

Meeks, Wayne A., gen. ed. *The HarperCollins Study Bible: New Revised Standard Version with the Apocryphal/Deuterocanonical Books*. New York: HarperCollins, 1993.

Metzger, Bruce M., and Coogan, Michael D., eds. *The Oxford Companion to the Bible*. New York: Oxford University Press, 1993.

Metzger, Bruce M., and Murphy, Roland E., eds. *The New Oxford Annotated Bible with the Apocryphal/Deuterocanonical Books*. New York: Oxford University Press, 1991.

Meyers, Carol L. *Discovering Eve: Ancient Israelite Women in Context*. New York: Oxford University Press, 1988.

_____. "Everyday Life: Women in the Period of the Hebrew Bible." In Newsom and Ringe, pp. 244-251.

Milgrom, Jacob. "Does the Bible Prohibit Homosexuality?" *Bible Review* 9, no. 6 (December 1993), 11.

Mühlberger, Richard. *The Bible in Art: The New Testament*. New York: Portland House, 1990.

_____. *The Bible in Art: The Old Testament*. New York: Portland House, 1991.

Murphy, Roland E. "Song of Songs, Book of." In Freeman v. 6, pp. 150-155.

_____. *The Tree of Life: An Exploration of Biblical Wisdom Literature*. New York: Doubleday, 1990.

Newsom, Carol A., and Ringe, Sharon H., eds. *The Women's Bible Commentary*. London: SPCK; Louisville, Ky: Westminster/John Knox Press, 1992.

Niditch, Susan. "Eroticism and Death in the Tale of Jael." In Day, pp. 43-57.

_____. "Genesis." In Newsom and Ringe, pp. 10-25.

O'Connor, Kathleen M. "Jeremiah." In Newsome and Ringe, pp. 169-177.

_____. "Lamentations." In Newsom and Ringe, pp. 178-182.

Oden, Robert A. *The Bible without Theology: The Theological Tradition and Alternatives to It*. San Francisco: Harper & Row, 1987.

Olyan, Saul M. *Asherah and the Cult of Yahweh in Israel.* Atlanta: Scholars Press, 1988.

Pagels, Elaine. *Adam, Eve, and the Serpent.* New York: Random House, 1988.

_____. *The Gnostic Gospels.* New York: Random House, 1979.

Pantel, Pauline Schmitt, ed. *A History of Women in the West: From Ancient Goddesses to Christian Saints.* Cambridge, MA: Harvard University Press.

Pardes, Ilana. *Countertraditions in the Bible: A Feminist Approach.* Cambridge, MA: Harvard University Press, 1992.

Patai, Raphael. *Sex and Family in the Bible and the Middle East.* Garden City, NY: Doubleday, 1959.

Phipps, William E. *Genesis and Gender: Biblical Myths of Sexuality and Their Cultural Impact.* New York: Praeger, 1989.

_____. *Was Jesus Married? The Distortion of Sexuality in the Christian Tradition.* New York: Harper & Row, 1970.

Pope, Marvin H. *Song of Songs: A New Translation with Introduction and Commentary* (The Anchor Bible 7C). Garden City, NY: Doubleday, 1977.

Pritchard, James B., ed. *Ancient Near Eastern Texts Relating to the Old Testament.* 3d ed. Princeton, NJ: Princeton University Press, 1969.

Riddle, John M.; Estes, J. Worth; and Russell, Josiah C. "Ever Since Eve... Birth Control in the Ancient World." *Archaeology* 47, no. 2 (March/April 1994), 29-35.

Ringe, Sharon H. "When Women Interpret the Bible." In Newsom and Ringe, pp. 1-9.

Robinson, James M., ed. *The Nag Hammadi Library in English.* Rev. ed. New York: HarperCollins, 1990.

Ruether, Rosemary Radford. *Womanguides: Readings Toward a Feminist Theology.* Boston: Beacon Press, 1985.

Russell, Letty M., ed. *Feminist Interpretation of the Bible.* Philadelphia: Westminster Press, 1985.

_____, ed. *The Liberating Word: A Guide to Nonsexist Interpretation of the Bible.* Philadelphia: Westminster Press, 1976.

Schaberg, Jane. *The Illegitimacy of Jesus.* New York: Crossroad,

1990.

Schaberg, Jane. "Luke." In Newsom and Ringe, pp. 275-292.

Schiffman, Lawrence H., and Achtemeier, Paul J. "Marriage." In Achtemeier, pp. 608-609.

Setel, Drorah O'Donnell. "Abortion." In Metzger and Coogan, p. 4.

_____. "Exodus." In Newsom and Ringe, pp. 26-35.

_____. "Prophets and Pornography: Female Sexual Imagery in Hosea." In Russell 1985, pp. 86-95.

Sissa, Giulia. "The Sexual Philosophies of Plato and Aristotle." In Pantel, pp. 46-81.

Smith, Morton, and Hoffmann, R. Joseph, eds. *What the Bible Really Says*. New York: HarperCollins, 1993.

Spong, John Shelby. *Born of a Woman: A Bishop Rethinks the Birth of Jesus*. San Francisco: HarperSanFrancisco, 1992.

Thiering, Barbara. *Jesus and the Riddle of the Dead Sea Scrolls: Unlocking the Secrets of His Life Story*. San Francisco: HarperSan Francisco, 1992.

Toorn, Karel van der. "Prostitution (Cultic)." In Freeman v. 5, pp. 510-513.

Trible, Phyllis. *God and the Rhetoric of Sexuality*. Philadelphia: Fortress Press, 1978.

_____. *Texts of Terror: Literary-Feminist Readings of Biblical Narratives*. Philadelphia: Fortress Press, 1984.

Turner, Nigel, the Rev. "Revelation." In Black and Rowley, pp. 1043-1061.

Unterman, Jeremiah. "Isaac." In Achtemeier, pp. 425-426.

Weems, Renita J. "Song of Songs." In Newsom and Ringe, pp. 156-160.

Wegner, Judith Romney. "Leviticus." In Newsom and Ringe, pp. 36-44.

Williams, The Rev. Robert. *Just As I Am: A Practical Guide to Being Out, Proud, and Christian*. New York: Crown, 1992.

Wilson, Ian. *Jesus: The Evidence*. San Francisco: Harper & Row, 1984.

Wolkstein, Diane, and Kramer, Samuel Noah. *Inanna, Queen*

of Heaven and Earth: Her Stories and Hymns from Sumer.
New York: Harper & Row, 1983.

Yee, Gale A. "Hosea." In Newsom and Ringe, pp. 195-202.

Name and Subject Index

Scripture Index